"Brexit" as a Social and Political Crisis

Through a focus on media and political discourses both before and after the UK 2016 EU Referendum, this volume provides a set of comprehensive, empirically based analyses of Brexit as a social and political crisis. The book explores a variety of context-dependent, ideologically driven, social, political, and economic imaginaries that have been attached to the idea/concept of Brexit in the UK and internationally.

The volume's wider contribution has three dimensions. First, it provides evidence of how the Brexit referendum debate and its immediate reactions were discursively framed and made sense of by a variety of social and political actors and through different media. Second, the contributors show how such discourses were reflexive of the wider path-dependent historical and political processes which have been instrumental in pre-defining the key pathways along which Brexit has been articulated. Third, the book identifies key patterns of national and international framing in order to discover the key, recurrent discursive trajectories in the ongoing process of Brexit – including after UK's formal departure from the EU in January 2020 – while putting forward an agenda for its further, in depth and systematic analysis in, in particular, politics and the media.

The chapters in this book were originally published as a special issue of *Critical Discourse Studies*.

Franco Zappettini is a Lecturer and Director of Postgraduate Research in Communication and Media at the University of Liverpool, UK. His research focuses on the textual/discursive analysis of different forms of political and organisational communication including mediated forms of populism, such as tabloid populism and Euroscepticism in the British press. He has published internationally in peer-reviewed journals. His latest publication is the monograph *European Identities in Discourse: A Transnational Citizens' Perspective* (2019).

Michał Krzyżanowski holds the Chair in Media and Communication Studies at Uppsala University, Sweden. He also remains affiliated to the Department of Communication & Media at the University of Liverpool, UK, and in 2018–19 he held the prestigious Albert Bonnier Jr. Guest Professorship in Media Studies at Stockholm University, Sweden. He is one of the leading international scholars working on critical discourse studies of race, ethnicity, and the politics of exclusion in the context of communication, media, and social change as well as of the challenges to democracy posed by the global rise of right-wing populism and neoliberalism. He is the Editor-in-Chief of the *Journal of Language and Politics* and a co-editor of the *Bloomsbury Advances in Critical Discourse Studies* in addition to sitting on a number of boards in various journals and book series.

"Brexit" as a Social and Political Crisis

Discourses in Media and Politics

Edited by
Franco Zappettini and Michał Krzyżanowski

Routledge
Taylor & Francis Group

LONDON AND NEW YORK

First published 2021
by Routledge
2 Park Square, Milton Park, Abingdon, Oxon, OX14 4RN

and by Routledge
605 Third Avenue, New York, NY 10158

Routledge is an imprint of the Taylor & Francis Group, an informa business

British Library Cataloguing-in-Publication Data
A catalogue record for this book is available from the British Library

ISBN13: 978-0-367-76411-1 (hbk)
ISBN13: 978-0-367-76412-8 (pbk)
ISBN13: 978-1-003-16683-2 (ebk)

Typeset in Myriad Pro
by codeMantra

Publisher's Note
The publisher accepts responsibility for any inconsistencies that may have arisen during the conversion of this book from journal articles to book chapters, namely the inclusion of journal terminology.

Disclaimer
Every effort has been made to contact copyright holders for their permission to reprint material in this book. The publishers would be grateful to hear from any copyright holder who is not here acknowledged and will undertake to rectify any errors or omissions in future editions of this book.

Contents

Citation Information

The chapters in this book were originally published in *Critical Discourse Studies*, volume 16, issue 4 (July 2019). When citing this material, please use the original page numbering for each article, as follows:

Chapter 6

For any permission-related enquiries please visit:
http://www.tandfonline.com/page/help/permissions

Contributors

Samuel Bennett is Assistant Professor at Adam Mickiewicz University in Poznań, Poland. He is a linguist and social scientist studying migrant integration, (non)belonging and exclusion, and populist politics. He is the author of *Constructions of Migrant Integration in British Public Discourse* (Bloomsbury, 2018) and has published widely in leading journals, including *Critical Discourse Studies* and the *Journal of Language & Politics*.

Michał Krzyżanowski holds the Chair in Media and Communication Studies at Uppsala University, Sweden. He is one of the leading international scholars working on critical discourse studies of race, ethnicity and the politics of exclusion in the context of communication, media and social change as well as of the challenges to democracy posed by the global rise of right-wing populism and neoliberalism. He is the Editor-in-Chief of the *Journal of Language and Politics* and a co-editor of the *Bloomsbury Advances in Critical Discourse Studies*.

Marzia Maccaferri is Associate Lecturer in Politics at Queen Mary as well as Goldsmiths, University of London, UK. Her research interests lie at the intersection of European political history (twentieth century) and intellectual history. Her work has a particular focus on the history of Italian and British intellectuals and on the relationship between intellectuals, public sphere, and journals and media.

Milica Pejovic is currently affiliated with the Université de Rennes 1, France, having completed her PhD at the School of International Studies of the University of Trento, Italy in 2019. Her research interests focus on Euroscepticism, EU communication policies, and the impact of new media on the contestation over EU policies and politics.

Carlo Ruzza is Professor of Political Sociology at the University of Trento, Italy, where he teaches courses on European and International Politics and on Political Sociology. He has previously taught at the Universities of Leicester, Essex, and Surrey – UK. His research interests focus upon populism, social movements, and right-wing parties. He is also interested in advocacy processes at European level, which include a focus on the efforts of civil society groups to affect policy-making in areas such as EU anti-discrimination policy and environmental policy.

Andrew Tolson was formerly Professor of Media and Communication at De Montfort University, Leicester, UK, and Honorary Visiting Fellow in the Department of Media and Communication at the University of Leicester, UK. He is also a founder member of the Ross Priory broadcast talk seminar (University of Strathclyde, Glasgow, UK). Since 2012 his work has concentrated on aspects of political communication and most recently, the uses of populist discourse in UK television journalism.

Franco Zappettini is a Lecturer and Director of Postgraduate Research in Communication and Media at the University of Liverpool, UK, where he also leads the module on Language and Media. His research focuses on the textual/discursive analysis of different forms of political and organisational communication including mediated forms of populism, such as tabloid populism and Euroscepticism in the British press.

Introduction – The critical juncture of Brexit in media & political discourses: from national-populist imaginary to cross-national social and political crisis

Franco Zappettini ⓘ and Michał Krzyżanowski ⓘ

1. Introduction

While the exact nature of Britain's exit from the EU – or 'Brexit' as it has been popularised – is still as unclear as whether it will take place at all, the complex ontology, unfolding and impact of such an unprecedented event have been investigated widely in several academic fields and especially in the sizeable body of work at the intersection of sociological, political and communicative dimensions (see for example, Clarke & Newman, 2017; Evans & Menon, 2017; Koller, Kopf, & Miglbauer, 2019; Ridge-Newman, Leon-Solis, & O'Donnell, 2018; Outhwaite, 2017; Wincott, Peterson, & Convery, 2017).

While our special issue joins the existent studies, it also differs from such work by specifically taking a critical discursive perspective. In doing so, we rely on an interpretation of Brexit as a 'critical juncture' (see below) in which different historical and contingent discursive nexuses and trajectories have been at play. Hence, we focus on the interplay between socio-political contexts as well as, therein, on various patterns of discursive work of both mediatisation and politicisation of Brexit, both before and after the UK 2016 EU Referendum. Through our focus, we explore a variety of context-dependent, ideologically-driven social, political and economic imaginaries that were attached to the idea/concept of Brexit and related notions in the process of their discursive articulation and legitimation in the UK and internationally.

Our contribution has thus three interrelated aims. First, the articles in this special issue provide evidence of how the Brexit referendum debate and its immediate reactions were discursively framed and made sense of by a variety of social and political actors and through different media. Second, we show how such discourses reflect the wider path-dependent historical and political processes which have been instrumental in defining the discursive and mediatic contexts within which Brexit has been articulated. Third, we identify discursive trajectories at play in the ongoing process of Brexit putting forward an agenda for further analysis of such trajectories.

2. The critical juncture of Brexit

The notion of critical juncture is well established in political studies and institutional theory and refers to 'situations of uncertainty in which decisions of important actors are causally decisive for the selection of one path of institutional development over other possible paths' (Capoccia, 2016; see also Zappettini, 2019b). In this sense, junctures are regarded as 'critical' because they set in motion path-dependent processes – in other words self-reinforcing trajectories – that become difficult to reverse as they eventually consolidate into one specific dominant institutional setup. At the same time, in a critical juncture, the contingent context in which choices are debated and made can also be seen as the result of institutional, cultural, and political trajectories which are reliant on antecedent conditions.

But nominally and more widely, the notion of critical juncture also corresponds to the idea that connects 'critique and crisis' (Koselleck, 1979; Krzyżanowski, 2019) pointing to the fact that – whether imagined or real – critical moments of history entail acceleration of discursive articulations of various visions of social reality as well as of their ideological foundation and legitimation. At such phases of a critical juncture, collective 'scope of experience' and 'horizon of expectations' (Koselleck, 2004) coagulate into various visions of collective past and future that give rise to patterns of understanding of the new, emergent social status quo. Rather than emerging as a discrete event, therefore, a critical juncture is more likely to consist of an accumulation of related events leading to a rapid social, political and institutional change. Of course, such events are ultimately driven by human agents, their ideologies, their interests and by the discourses through which specific choices are advocated and deliberation over such choices are made.

Drawing on the above, in this special issue we hence approach Brexit as a critical juncture 'in the making'. We see Brexit emerging at the intersection of different path-dependent discursive trajectories which have accumulated 'forces, antagonisms and contradictions' (Clarke & Newman, 2017, p. 102) over a period of time and have resulted in the contingency of the 2016 referendum in which British voters were asked to decide whether to leave or remain in the European Union. To paraphrase Capoccia and Kelemen (2007) who – taking up Berlin (1974) – define contingency as 'the study of what happened in the context of what could have happened' (p. 355), this special issue hence examines discourses of Brexit as 'what was said in the context of what could have been said'. Our interest thus is not in language use *per se,* but rather in discursive practices as vehicles of different attitudes and ideologies. We therefore appeal to discourses as wider perspectives and as specific entry points for the analysis. They help us explore how some of the linguistic and semiotic productions surrounding the contingency of the Brexit referendum relate to different path-dependent trajectories and how these discourses have been articulated and seized upon by different actors at the time of the said critical juncture. For example, in its contingent form, Brexit has been a process defined by political opportunism aimed at reigning in the infight over Europe inside the Conservative Party but, in turn, such process have been fuelled by long-standing trajectories of British imperialism and Euroscepticism rooted in the historical visions of the relationship between Britain and the 'continent' and in the perceived distinct history of the British Empire and its democratic traditions from wider Europe (see, in particular, Maccaferri, 2019).

The contingency of the 2016 Referendum on Brexit has also involved the (re)articulation of social, political and cultural narratives along logics of *rupture, continuity* or, in some cases, contradictorily both (Zappettini, 2019a). At institutional level, for example, discourses of 'one United Kingdom' which downplayed or even silenced the gamut of different regional views of Brexit across England, Scotland, Wales, and Northern Ireland were contrasted by narratives of rupture with the EU as an institutional framework politically and economically incompatible with Britain and its trade ambitions. At the same time, however, the institutional rhetoric has also portrayed new 'global' Britain as committed to 'shared European values' as the UK 'leaves the EU but not Europe' (see Krzyżanowski, 2010 for the ambivalent discursive constructions of the EU and Europe) and as the government vision for an out-of-the-EU UK has gradually shifted from 'ambitious' to 'pragmatic'.

The Brexit referendum was also – or perhaps in particular – reasserted and articulated through a discursive contingency based on the simplistic antagonism of the in/out binaries. These binaries were discursively appropriated by different actors and, in turn, they indexed larger ideological struggles over key political and social issues. For example, Brexit has been interpreted in relation to an international surge in populist backlash against globalisation and Europeanization as the perceived causes of rapid social changes (Calhoun, 2017). In this sense, for many 'Leavers', Brexit embodied the perceived opportunity for Britain to shift away from an 'unavoidable' supranational path inside the EU back to a 'safer' (inter)national system of relations. However, the Leave campaign 'take back control' slogan often represented a floating signifier that instrumentally legitimised both a logic of *global deceleration* rejecting neoliberalism and austerity (through the argument that power taken over by the EU global governance project should be reigned back into national remits) and a logic of *global acceleration* advocating further liberalisation and international free trade (through the argument that EU regulations prevent the UK from taking full advantage of worldwide economic opportunities) (cf. Zappettini, 2019a, 2019b).

3. Unpacking discourses of Brexit: contributions in this special issue

The contributions to this special issue reflect the multilevel, actor-specific discursive trajectories that have characterised Brexit as a mediated critical juncture. The first article by Maccaferri (2019) sets the scene by taking a historical perspective and tracing how British political discourse has traditionally constructed the relation between the UK and the 'continent' as an uncomfortable one. Analysing a corpus of traditional and online press coverage of the referendum, Maccaferri suggests that, along with interpretations of Brexit as a rejection of the élite, of austerity policies, and of globalisation, the thrust of the referendum debate was found in the recontextualisation of Eurosceptic discourses that have been circulating in British politics since the 1960s and which, in turn, are rooted in the historical idea of the British Empire. The press portrayal of this renewed belief in the nation's future, Maccaferri claims, was a significant driver of the Brexit vote as well as an expression of resurgent English (rather than British) populism.

In the second contribution, Zappettini (2019b) investigates the discourses of the two organisations designated by the UK Electoral Commission as the official lead campaigns for the 'leave' and 'remain' vote, focusing on the institutional framing of the referendum debate and on the structural conditions that allowed for the emergence and legitimisation of the in/out camps. For Zappettini, the discursive opportunities created by the institutional framework effectively enabled these two actors to fill the 'Brexit' signifier with specific and selected signifieds and to simplistically associate such meanings with the contingency of the in/out referendum binary. From this perspective, his analysis provides evidence of the key themes that gained traction in the public arena, namely trade and immigration. As Zappettini argues, despite adopting different argumentative positions, the two actors largely framed the Brexit debate within representations of the Single Market and of Europe as a zero-sum trading exercise whilst civic and transnational discourses of European solidarity were notably absent. In the case of Vote Leave, the 'moral panic' constructed around immigration proved a key narrative – albeit premised on fallacies and misrepresentations – which, Zappettini suggests, ultimately has legitimised Brexit along a toxic logic of new mercantilism, nation-centric imaginaries and rejection of the 'other'.

Tolson's (2019) contribution adopts the perspective of journalistic practices to highlight how anonymous *vox pops* featuring in TV reports during and after the referendum campaign became highly newsworthy 'soundbites' that contributed to the legitimation of Brexit as a choice of/for the people. More importantly, for Tolson, by reproducing stereotypical representation of 'ordinary' voters, the media had a pivotal role in the construction of Brexit as a populist scenario. As Tolson critically suggests, the news agenda that drove Brexit fed specific narratives of division, for example by representing social and cultural distances between the disengaged Leavers in rural and industrial Britain on one side and the Westminster-based metropolitan elites of politicians and journalists on the other. Tolson argues that eventually the journalistic use of vox pops contributed to a convergence between such populist discourses and a normalisation of their reproduction in the public sphere.

A similar reading of Brexit from populist and public sphere perspectives is offered by Ruzza and Pejovic (2019) who analyze the cultural frames that most frequently characterised interpretations of Brexit in Facebook posts addressed to the EU Commission and the European Parliament immediately after the referendum. Likening this virtual context of production of discourses to a transnational arena of debate where mobilisation around Brexit arises similarly to social movement dynamics, Ruzza and Pejovic's analysis interprets Brexit as part of an emerging (pan-European) populist ideology that pits the 'elite' against 'the people'. In this case, the authors suggest that in Facebook posts, the frame of 'the EU elites as culprits' was frequently underpinning the logic of Brexit, with different categories of actors – such as national politicians, financial institutions and multinational corporations – conveniently conflated with the EU institutions and juxtaposed with 'ordinary people'. Similarly, democratic deficit and the understanding of Brexit as a restoration of British freedom were powerful discursive drivers for Leavers. Ruzza and Pejovic suggest that while frames referring to the legitimacy of supranational governance were prevalent in the posts, discourses of migration and the economy (the key arguments of the official Leave/Remain campaigns) were relatively less significant in the dataset analyzed. Another point raised by Ruzza and Pejovic is that whilst the transnational space of debate was open to everyone, the majority of active participants were (pro-Brexit) British. As the authors suggest, this may indicate the historic British insular attitudes may in fact have been traded off for the political opportunity of a new ideological anti-cosmopolitan coalition coalesced around the Brexit vote.

In the following contribution, Bennett (2019) contends that the narration of crisis was pivotal in the Brexit campaign. Focusing on a televised debate broadcast by the BBC close to the referendum date, Bennett traces frames and linguistic features deployed by cross-party representative of the two coalitions trying to persuade 'floating' voters. Bennett's key argument is that the vote over Brexit was discursively positioned as a 'turning point' in what was narrated by both Leave and Remain sides as a crisis. In the author's analysis, for Leavers the crisis was already present and the solution they envisaged was to leave the EU and thereby remove the threats/problems associated with it (exemplified by the topos of taking control). Conversely, for Remainers the crisis would in fact be triggered by the choice of leaving the EU. Bennett suggests that both sides invoked general crisis scenarios which, in turn, recontextualised discourses of other crises, namely immigration, sovereignty, economy and public services. Significantly, Bennett highlights how, while discourses articulated in the televised debate were polarised around the remain/leave split, they cut across different political affiliations in a temporary suspension of traditional partisan alignment.

Finally, Krzyżanowski (2019) offers further evidence of how different representations of crises (whether real or imagined) sustained the framing of Brexit in/by the international press. In a comparative study covering four European countries with different levels of engagement with the European project (Austria, Germany, Poland and Sweden), Krzyżanowski shows how both the liberal and conservative press of these countries, unlike most of the British press, represented Brexit as both a current and a future 'real' crisis placing different emphasis on its social, political and economic implications. However, while his analysis suggests a convergence of discourses towards an international and a European (public sphere) reading of Brexit, Krzyżanowski also highlights the significant degree of domestication of news of Brexit across the four national dimensions especially in relation to neoliberally-framed economic and Eurosceptic discourses that clearly gained increased traction even in the seemingly pro-European liberal and conservative media.

4. Tracing the discursive trajectories of Brexit. A critical discourse studies agenda for future analysis

Although the Brexit juncture is still in the making, the contributions in this issue have highlighted some overarching themes and pointed to how Brexit has been discursively consolidating around a number of intersecting ideologically-anchored trajectories.

The first emergent trajectory encompasses a large proportion of *discourses driven by populist and nationalist ideologies*. As we have shown, the Brexit debate was typically framed in antagonistic terms, whether through representations of 'us' and 'them', 'cosmopolitan' vs. 'rural', 'ordinary people' vs. the 'elite', 'Europe' vs. 'Britain' and so on (see contributions by Tolson, 2019; Ruzza & Pejovic, 2019). Of course, the resurgence of populist and nationalist discourses is not simply a Brexit-specific or a uniquely British phenomenon but a multi-faceted one that has wider European and worldwide dimensions (see for example Krzyżanowski, 2018; Krzyżanowski, Triandafyllidou, & Wodak, 2018; Wodak & Krzyżanowski, 2017). This calls for an examination of cross-national as well as localised forms of such discursive trajectories and their interplay with the unfolding of Brexit. For example, we have seen how many discursive manifestations of Brexit encapsulated an ideological shift from a political, economic and cultural order of supranational and multilateral relations to a world order based on national independence and neoliberal intergovern-mentalism, a reverse of Fukuyama's (2006) prediction on the 'end of history'. It will be important to follow how these discourses play out in relation to future choices of the British government over the new relationship with the EU and other countries, which future trade and social policies will be adopted after Brexit and what their impact will be. It will be equally important to continue investigating the patterns of populist and nationalist legitimation of Brexit in a wider sense (see also below) along with the surely still forthcoming further attempts to package the national 'wilful self-harm' (O'Toole, 2018) as it is in discourses of post-imperialist success and grandeur.

The second discursive trajectory that we bring attention to is that of political crisis. Not only has the *notion of crisis* (both external and internal to the UK) represented a powerful anchor around which many discourses of Brexit unfolded during the referendum in the UK and internationally (see articles by Bennett, 2019; Krzyżanowski, 2019) but ideological struggles around such discourses have also contributed to major changes in the British political landscape. In this respect, while the Brexit vote notably tallied with working class voters drifting away from traditional Labour links and towards the Conservative party and UKIP, the ideological Leave/Remain split has now transcended the traditional left/right divide in British politics (see Bennett, 2019). Moreover, ideological struggles over the execution of Brexit have precipitated the UK and its constituent countries into a constitutional crisis over the power of Parliament, the function of democracy, and the remits of national and regional sovereignty which is likely to have profound repercussions in the short and long term.

The third discursive trajectory that will require close examination is the process of *legitimation of Brexit*. As we have shown, the referendum was part of a discursive chain through which discourses that had emerged on the fringe of politics (but historically rooted) gradually climbed up the institutional chain to become normalised into the language of government. This process has been sustained by different discursive tools, for example the tautology of 'Brexit means Brexit' and the rhetorical appeal to the 'will/voice of the people'. The latter, in particular, has become a key discursive driver and an ambivalent signifier of democratic and populist chains of legitimation and *pre-legitimation* (Krzyża-nowski, 2014) that are defining the struggle around the 'privileged sign' of Brexit, especially as the 'will of the people' is being discursively retrofitted to the promises of the referendum campaign, thus gaining legitimacy not only by its moral virtue but also specific path-dependency (Leeuwen, 2007). But, as we show, the legitimation of Brexit has also been fuelled by various *discursive shifts* (Krzyżanowski, 2018) at the institutional level and in public discourses. For example, the UK Government has shifted from an initial position of no compromise with the EU ('no deal is better than a bad deal') to that of cooperation ('a deep and special partnership') and while themes of immigration were prominent during the campaign, the current public debate seems to be more focused on future trade arrangements as the 'bottom line' logic of Brexit.

In taking into account all these discursive dynamics, one can hardly underestimate the role of media in (re)producing and framing such discourses as well as creating wider path-dependencies eventually followed by the wider social and political discourse. Whether it be traditional or new forms of communication (e.g. traditional press, televised debates, online campaigns or Facebook posts), our contributors have provided ample evidence of how Brexit has been a mediated and multi-actor process.

Crucially, Brexit is yet an unfinished process. At the time of writing many uncertainties are still surrounding the so called 'end state' of Brexit, including the final shape of the trade relationship between Britain and the EU, the status of EU citizens in Britain and that of British citizens in the EU as well as the thorny issue of the Irish border, or indeed whether Brexit will occur at all. The plethora of discourses through which these issues are being (re)articulated and (de)legitimised represents a vantage point for any scholar who aims to make sense of Brexit by providing insightful and robust analysis. In keeping with the Critical Discourse Studies orientation of discourse as 'text in context', in this issue we have argued for and provided empirical application of an examination of Brexit as a critical juncture in the making occurring at the intersection of historical, political and mediated dimensions. We encourage future research that will systematically explore both the micro discursive sites where discourses of Brexit are produced and consumed by different actors– e.g. media, government, civil society –and the path dependency trajectories that such discourses create and feed on.

Disclosure statement

No potential conflict of interest was reported by the authors.

ORCID

Franco Zappettini http://orcid.org/0000-0001-7049-4454
Michal Krzyzanowski http://orcid.org/0000-0003-4073-2831

References

Bennett, S. (2019). Present tense, future (im)perfect: 'Brexit' as a crisis issue in UK political discourse. *Critical Discourse Studies*, in press.

Berlin, I. (1974). Historic inevitability. In P. Gardiner (Ed.), *The philosophy of history* (pp. 161–186). Oxford: Oxford University Press.

Calhoun, C. (2017). Populism, nationalism and Brexit. In W. Outhwaite (Ed.), *Brexit: Sociological responses* (pp. 57–76). London; New York: Anthem Press.

Capoccia, G. (2016). Critical junctures. In O. Fioretos, T. Falleti, & A. Sheingate (Eds.), *The Oxford handbook of historical institutionalism* (pp. 89–106). Oxford: Oxford University Press.

Capoccia, G., & Kelemen, D. (2007). The study of critical junctures: Theory, narrative, and counterfactuals in historical institutionalism. *World Politics, 59*(3), 341–369.

Clarke, J., & Newman, J. (2017) 'People in this country have had enough of experts': Brexit and the paradoxes of populism. *Critical Policy Studies, 11*(1), 101–116.

Evans, G., & Menon, A. (2017). *Brexit and British politics*. London: Polity Press.

Fukuyama, F. (2006). *The end of history and the last man*. New York: Free Press, Simon and Schuster.

Koller, V., Kopf, S., & Miglbauer, M. (Eds.). (2019). *Discourses of Brexit*. London: Routledge.

Koselleck, R. (1979). *Critique and crisis*. Cambridge, MA: MIT Press.

Koselleck, R. (2004). *Futures past: On the semantics of historical time*. New York, NY: Columbia University Press.

Krzyżanowski, M. (2010). *The discursive construction of European identities*. Frankfurt: Peter Lang.

Krzyżanowski, M. (2014). Values, imaginaries and templates of journalistic practice: A critical discourse analysis. *Social Semiotics, 24*(3), 345–365.

Krzyżanowski, M. (2018). Discursive shifts in ethno-nationalist politics: On politicization and mediatization of the "refugee crisis" in Poland. *Journal of Immigrant & Refugee Studies, 16*(1–2), 76–96.

Krzyżanowski, M. (2019). Brexit and the imaginary of 'crisis': A discourse-conceptual analysis of European news media. *Critical Discourse Studies*, in press.

Krzyżanowski, M., Triandafyllidou, A., & Wodak, R. (Eds.). (2018). The mediatization and politicization of the refugee crisis in Europe. *Journal of Immigrant and Refugee Studies, 16*, 1–14. London: Routledge.

Leeuwen, T. V. (2007). Legitimation in discourse and communication. *Discourse & Communication, 1* (1), 91–112. doi:10.1177/1750481307071986

Maccaferri, M. (2019). Splendid isolation again? Brexit and the role of the press and online media in re-narrating the European discourse. *Critical Discourse Studies*, in press.

O'Toole, F. (2018). *Heroic failure: Brexit and the politics of pain*. London: Head of Zeus.

Outhwaite, W. (2017). *Brexit: Sociological responses*. London: Anthem Press.

Ridge-Newman, A., Leon-Solis, F., & O'Donnell, H. (Eds.). (2018). *Reporting the road to Brexit*. Basingstoke: Palgrave Macmillan.

Ruzza, C., & Pejovic, M. (2019). 'Populism at work: The language of the Brexiteers and the European Union'. *Critical Discourse Studies*, in press.

Tolson, A. (2019). "Out is out and that's it the people have spoken": Uses of vox pops in UK TV news coverage of the Brexit referendum. *Critical Discourse Studies*, in press.

Wincott, D., Peterson, J., & Convery, A. (2017). Introduction: Studying Brexit's causes and consequences. *The British Journal of Politics and International Relations, 19*(3), 429–433.

Wodak, R., & Krzyżanowski, M. (Eds.). (2017). Right-wing populism in Europe and the USA: Contesting politics and discourse beyond 'orbanism' and 'trumpism'. *Journal of Language and Politics, 16*, 471–484.

Zappettini, F. (2019a). The official vision for 'global Britain': Brexit as rupture and continuity between free trade, liberal internationalism and 'values'. In V. Koller, S. Kopf, & M. Milgbauer (Eds.), *Discourses of Brexit* (pp. 140–154). Abingdon: Routledge.

Zappettini, F. (2019b). The Brexit referendum: How trade and immigration in the discourses of the official campaigns have legitimised a toxic (inter)national logic. *Critical Discourse Studies*, in press.

Splendid isolation again? Brexit and the role of the press and online media in re-narrating the European discourse

Marzia Maccaferri

ABSTRACT

Europe as an idea as well as a political and cultural project has been a vast subject in the British public debate, The relationship between Britain and Europe was mostly regarded as extremely cautious and parochially nationalist; however, whereas in the 1960s and 1970s opposition to the European Economic Community (ECC) was predominantly led by intelligentsias and maverick politicians, the present-day debate seems less intellectually-driven and academic in his language. This article draws attention to the role of traditional and online media in re-narrating the European question. Within this process, the re-semioticization of the role of Great Britain in the international scenario vis-à-vis the historical and cultural discourses of borders between the UK and the Continent play a pivotal function. Starting from here, the article considers, on the one hand, how the current re-narration of the European question is reproducing and reinterpreting historical arguments vis-à-vis old clichés. On the other, it deals primarily with the response to the profound transition taking place in the political landscape.

Introduction. Brexit: a historical and conceptual puzzle

The European question has been one of the most controversial and debated issue in British politics since the Second World War; the result of the referendum of 23 June 2016 has inexorably marked a new phase in the troubled relationship between Britain and the rest of Europe. The implications of Brexit are extremely transformative, and an increasingly growing body of scholarship has emerged exploring the causes that have led to the decision to leave the EU and its consequences (see among others, Blagden, 2017; Clarke, Goodwin, & Whiteley, 2017; Diamond, Nedergaard, & Rosamond, 2018; Freeden, 2017; Inglehart & Norris, 2016; Wincott, 2017; Wincott, Peterson, & Convey, 2017. Also, see the first accounts in the field of media studies: Jackson, Thorsen, & Wring, 2016; Levy, Aslan, & Bironzo, 2016).

Focusing principally on a short-term perspective, these studies have mainly concentrated on the electoral analysis and to what extent the United Kingdom's decision reflected trends toward populism already witnessed in Europe (Albertazzi & McDonnel, 2015) or system-challenging politics (see also Wilson, 2017). A different strand has converged on the dialectic between cosmopolitanism and transnationalism (see Hopkin, 2017; Outhwaite, 2017), clearly encompassing the Brexit phenomenon within the more general framework of neoliberalism and its 'hegemonic mode of discourse' (Harvey, 2005; Schulz-Forberg & Olsen, 2014).

Brexit is markedly complex to read and comprehensive interpretations are hard to draw. As this article suggests, it would be helpful to deconstruct Brexit discourse using a broader long-term historical approach. British discourse on Europe's political project has always been uneasy and uncomfortable (Bogdanor, 2005; Daddow, 2004; Grob-Fitzgibbon, 2016; Marquand, 2008). However, in the last few decades Europe has been seen as an extraneous 'overseas' corpus rather than a political process, thus inducing a 'reaction to' it instead of an 'action upon' its policies (Westlake, 2017). A closer look at the historical construction of the European question in the British debate and its *operational* links with the public discourse during the referendum campaign illustrates how the Brexit discourse was actually an ongoing 'recontextualization' of traditional historical narratives. This re-narration reproduced historical arguments as well as reinterpreted dated clichés to finally create a new hierarchal discursive order.

Drawing from Krzyżanowski's reading of the notion of recontextualisation theorised by Basil Bernstein, this article therefore considers the Brexit discourse not only as a process of repositioning of arguments and ideas across spatio-temporal scales, but first and foremost, as a process of creating new horizontal discourse orderings and a new hegemony of discursive frames (Krzyżanowski, 2016, p. 314). This was an act of ideological formation of discursive shifts and, as this article argues, its analysis will benefit from a concept-oriented examination. According to Krzyżanowski (2013, 2016), the increasing conceptualisation of contemporary public discourse needs to hybridise the theoretical and analytical apparatus of critical discourse analysis (CDS) with a concept-oriented historical method. Rather than looking at the Brexit phenomenon through the lens of its potential misrepresentation, whose centrality however has been accurately highlighted by most of the recent political science scholarship, this article will read the conceptual nature of Brexit as a process of discursive construction and recontextualisation at the intersection of various semantic fields.

Starting from the conceptual history framework (Koselleck, 1988; Müller, 2014; Stråth & Wodak, 2009), and building on Discourse-Historical Analysis (DHA) (Krzyżanowski, 2010; Wodak & Meyer, 2009), this article examines both traditional and online media coverage as a principal indicator of public discourse, representing a meta-narrative of the public debate by mirroring, selecting and processing the puzzle of topics and narratives upon which public discourse revolved. Among other agencies of discursive power (Stråth, 2006), the traditional press, bolstered by online media, still holds a crucial role in shaping British public opinion in general (Balch & Balabanova, 2017) and, more specifically, Brexit discourse. Historically, British public opinion has always turned to the newspapers at times of national significance and national crisis (Greenslade, 2004). Indeed, the Brexit vote confirms this propensity: according to the June 2016 Audit Bureau of Circulation (ABC) figures, almost 3 million more national newspapers were sold during the last month of the referendum campaign.[1]

This conceptual framework is developed in the following three sections of the article. First there is a historical contextualisation of the troubled relationship between the United Kingdom and the European project. Then, the historical discourse of Brexit is put to work via a thematic analysis of the press; the interdiscursivity of the Brexit discourse concludes this section. The results of this analysis are presented and discussed in the conclusion.

My main aim is to showcase that the Brexit discourse and the recontextualisation of the UK-EU relationship together present a dramatic change and seem highly indicative of a new ideological and intra-party cleavage that could transform the British political system: from an élitist debate – 1960s–1970s narratives on Europe were predominantly led by intellectuals and intelligentsias, using an academic language – to populistic arguments and tones. Does this shift (re)create a British nationalistic identity based upon a new post-imperial exceptionalism and the Anglo-sphere's hegemony?

Britain and Europe: a troubled relationship

Apart from the 'transient infatuation' with Europe of the first Tony Blair government (Daddow, 2013), and the passionate struggle of Edward Heath – the Prime Minister who signed the treaty admitting the UK to the European Communities in 1972 – the relationship between Britain and the European Community has been mostly regarded as cautious and parochial. The perceptions of Britain's (Imperial) past and the national historical narrative have played a major role. On the one hand, the self-representation of Britain (meaning, more often, England) as *the* ideally Liberal and democratic nation first shaped by the Reformation, the Industrial Revolution and later framed by Victorian values has created a national identity clearly detached from the Continent. On the other, this Victorian sense of 'splendid isolation'[2] was extensively reinforced by the experiences of World War Two (Harrison, 2009) to the extent that there is no substantial difference between the famous headlines in *The Times* 'Dense fog in the Channel: Continent isolated for three days' (1939) and 'Fog in the Channel – Continent cut off' (1957). Although in terms of transnational cultural relations, English 'isolationism' and its sense of 'uniqueness' should not be exaggerated – England and especially Scotland were very much part of the European intellectual and political networks from the seventeenth to the twentieth century –, nevertheless these ties were almost interpreted as a way to preserve Britain's influence (Bell, 2007; Parry, 2006).

The Suez crisis (1956) played a salient role for the formation of the post-imperial British national identity and its relationship with the idea of Europe. From 1956 onwards, Britain was immersed in a long and exhausting debate on the 'decline of the nation' (Tomlinson, 2009) while France, which emerged from the same international crisis with an adamant attitude towards the European project, Britain on the contrary flirted again with a newly materialised 'splendid isolation' (Maccaferri, 2009). In those years, almost all intellectuals and commentators, newspapers or weeklies labelled Britain as 'the sick man of Europe', which is *per se* ironic because it was a British voice, John Russel quoting Nicholas I of Russia, who invented that figure of speech in order to indicate Turkey's state of affairs during the Crimea war in the late nineteenth century (quoted in *The New York Times*, 12 May 1860). Forced by the collapse of the Empire and by the political irrelevance of the Commonwealth project, but above all pressed by a lagging economy as compared with the 'European economic miracles,' the UK finally joined the EEC in 1973.

Starting from the Suez crisis, therefore, the discourse on Europe revolved around two distinct but conflicting facets: on the one hand, Europe had been associated with the discourse of 'decline' and entangled with the ideology of 'declinism' (Daddow, 2013; Hall, 2012). The anxieties concerning Britain's international and economic future were compounded in the 1970s by the surge in local nationalism (Wales and Scotland) as epitomised by Tom Nairn's expression 'the break-up of Britain' (Nairn, 1977). The Europe narrated in the 1960s and 1970s, and especially during the infamous 'winter of discontent' (1978–79), was therefore perceived as *the* only condition to confront the new modernity and post-Fordist capitalism. The confrontational narratives of the Europe-Britain dyad were further inflamed by the byzantine discourse on Europe elaborated by Thatcherism in 1980s (Wright & Gamble, 2000). It is within this conundrum that we can trace the roots of contemporary Eurosceptic and Europhile discourses.

The UK's Eurosceptic discourse appeals to the nation's sense of pride and its imperial past, its military record and its parliamentary history: Britain as a world power and as a beacon of democracy. It plays upon wartime efforts and achievements. With noticeable differences between the decades, hostility to Europe and the EU springs from the assumption that British identity, British economic orientation and political traditions are not part of Europe's history and culture. A lesser element of the Eurosceptic discourse is based on religion, and on the idea of Europe as a capitalist product (Maccaferri, 2017). The Europhile discourse also calls on history to support its narrative but using the reverse argument: it is the history of Europe and the European project, its economic and relative international success that encourage Britain's involvement. Within this perspective Europe, therefore, represents a resolution to the economic decline, and embodies a discursive strategy towards 'modernity' (Daddow, 2013).

Both Eurosceptic and Europhile discourses rely predominantly on history as their starting point. Both discourses formulate their constructions and arguments on the back of competing perceptions of history, with different degrees of 'incommensurability' – taking here Thomas Kuhn's concept referring to the way in which different communities hold contrasting perceptions of a phenomenon (Daddow, 2004). Both discourses have been built upon history, 'depend on' history; but they problematise a different past. Historical narratives are constantly discursively (re)constructed and, according to Bourdieu (1993), dominant discourses and narratives tend to relativise, deny, reformulate or even bury dramatic events. This process of discursive engagement between two different pasts has gradually trivialised and oversimplified the Britain-Europe dyad.

During the aforementioned process not only has the Britain-Europe nexus undergone a repositioning of various elements of language and discourse across different sites of production and reception – from an academic topic, Europeanisation and its critique had become popular arguments (Varouxakis, 2010) – but, drawing here from Bernstein's extended concept, during their 'recontextualization' especially in the months of the referendum campaign, some discourses lost their primary function and became a new signifier for a new hegemonic discourse (Krzyżanowski, 2016). In this sense, as this article will show, the selective reproduction of historical narratives and discourses is a self-replicating process: it has decontextualised some concepts, rearranged and reshaped other elements in order to craft (new) strategic hierarchies and ideologies.

The historical discourse of Brexit in the press

The recontextualisation of the Britain-Europe dyad experienced a sharp acceleration during the Brexit referendum. As an example of how different historical narrations acquire different semantic fields over time, I have analysed Brexit discourse as constructed in the traditional and online British press. The coverage for this article focuses only on editorials and comments in the period between the announcement of the date of the referendum made by the Prime Minister David Cameron after the renegotiations on the UK's relationship with the EU (20 February 2016) and the day of the referendum (23 June 2016). Excluding the regional newspapers and the tabloids, my selection of sources was: *The Daily Telegraph* and *The Telegraph on Sunday*, *The Times* and *The Sunday Times*, *The Guardian* and *The Observer*, *The Financial Times*, *The Economist*, *New Statesmen*, *The Spectator*, *Prospect*, *Opendemocracy.com*. This selection generated a corpus of almost 1000 articles, most of which concentrated in May and June 2017 (see Table 1).

In framing the role of the newspapers' scene, it is important to distinguish, on the one hand, the short-term role newspaper discourse played during the referendum campaign which, mirroring a conflictual rather than collaborative relationship with the EU, oversimplified narratives and ideologies. On the other hand, it is also central to stress the long-term cumulative influence exercised by the media. The UK provides a paradigmatic case study with which to explore the discursive construction of Euroscepticism. According to Berry (in Jackson et al., 2016), well before the campaign began, the European discourse had been primed by the media to be Eurosceptic. In addition, the public opinion has a limited knowledge of the European politics and history and, by neglecting the peacetime dimensions of modern European history, the national historiography and the educational system retain a major responsibility in generating and sustaining the popularity of British Eurosceptic arguments (Daddow, 2006).

In terms of selection of sources, I chose to focus my attention on editorials and comments because they represent the main field to explore the interconnectivity between discourse – understood as the terrain in which reproducing/misrepresenting the society (Fairclough & Wodak, 1997) – and political concepts at the intersection between historical narrations and recontextualisation of the past (Stråth, 2006). To some extent, editorials and comments are independent cultural as well as political actors, representing the newspapers' collective opinion and intervening in the debate through 'declarations of editorial positions with the strategic aim of influencing politicians, campaigners and readers' (Firmstone, 2016, p. 36). In line with the HDA framing of my research, I have excluded tabloids because, although they still represent a pivotal instrument for the reordering of the public discourse in Britain, their meta-narrative nevertheless appears very simplistic, revolving more around

Table 1. UK press positioning during the Brexit Referendum campaign.

Brexit press *with editorial stance	Remain press *with editorial stance
Daily Telegraph and *Telegraph on Sunday* [*]	*Financial Times* [*]
Sunday Times [*]	*Guardian* and *Observer* [*]
Daily Mail [*]	*Times* [*]
Daily Express and *Sunday Express* [*]	/
Spectator	*Economist* [*]
	New Statesmen [*]
	Prospect [*]
	Opendemocracy.com

sensationalist front pages and pictures rather than concepts and context-specific arguments. On the contrary, the process of discursive recontextualization can be better deconstructed and analysed through the editorials and comments where it is possible to trace the overall logic of certain strands and its reproduction and intervention in the debate.

In line with my selection of sources, I draw the main analytical categories and following examples from a textual quality analysis of my corpus of editorials and comments. In the first stage I enucleate the main topics of the debate: immigration, economy, EU bureaucracy, borders. Each topic can be identified with a sort of catchphrase utilised by the press both as a positive argument or as a counterargument (see Table 2). The role played by the discourse of these topics was preparing the semantic field for the process of recontextualisation.

To introduce my argument, the *Leave* camp was intensely prominent, employing a compelling narrative capable of constructing a positive and proactive argument for leaving the EU via the general claim of 'regaining control.' This strong exposure forced the *Remain* media to chase after Brexit's arguments and, combined with a belated political determination to lead the *Remain* campaign (see 'Jeremy Corbyn, saboteur,' *The Economist*, 11 June 2016), the anti-Brexit camp patterned a 'negative' discourse mostly focused on warnings about the economic implications (so-called 'project fear'). The result was to reinforce the main Brexit arguments and, ultimately, contribute to the prominence of the macro narratives of auto-determination and control, sovereignty and security and thus marginalising social, cultural and civic issues. Although this time the situation in the UK was perceived as very different (the country's economic performance in 2016 was much healthier than those of countries in Continental Europe), this argument however reproposed in inverted terms the *topos* of 'declinism' that had framed the British discourse on Europe since its origins in the late 1950s:

Example 1

A simple message runs through all this; Europe is sliding into stagnation, turmoil and extremism. Britain must inoculate itself by getting out of the EU (or as Mr Hannan calls it: "the elderly, creaking, sclerotic economies on the Western tip of the Eurasian landmass") while it can, Europe has plenty of problem but such exaggerations will become yet more lurid as the campaign enters its final weeks [...]. The insinuation that Britain should abandon its neighbours of need – anti-democratic forces on the march, decline and disintegration threatening – is a betrayal of the blood, sweat and treasure that the country has dedicated to the pursuit of peace and prosperity on the continent ('The continental imperative,' *The Economist*, 28 May 2016).

There has been only one reliable way of reducing migration: recession (Eaton, 2016)

In terms of discourse topics, in addition to the economy, the other theme that featured most forcefully was 'immigration' (see Table 2). This is hardly surprising. Immigration from other European countries and its association with the Eurosceptic discourse, and

Table 2. Thematic analysis.

Topics	Thematic analysis
(a) *Immigration = 'taking back control'* (b) *Economy = getting rid of Brussels' bankers* (c) *EU bureaucracy = 'give us our money back'* (d) *Borders = English liberties*	(a) *Use of historical categories: 'British exceptionalism', 'splendid isolation', WW2 pride* (b) *The Pound as identity* (c) *Sovereignty and Parliament: English democracy* (d) *British = English*

the rise of populist political actors has been clearly acknowledged (Albertazzi & McDonnel, 2015; Moffitt, 2016; Müller, 2016). Moreover, according to Balch and Balabanova (2016), a significant swing in the use of welfare chauvinist arguments (economic nationalism) and the need to restrict free movement on the basis of public security had been already recorded between 2006 and 2013. It is clear from my findings that this trend reached its apex in the last two months before the referendum (see Example 2). While before the climax of the campaign, the free movement was primarily understood through a more balanced argument based on the consequence in terms of costs and benefits (utilitarianism) as testified by Balch and Balabanova (2016), during the referendum campaign 'immigration' was nevertheless increasingly reported as a 'threat' to the United Kingdom in its dramatic variations as a menace for the British welfare system (see also a more accurate analysis of the prominence of 'economy' and 'immigration' news published in Jackson et al., 2016).

Example 2

Europe is expecting a similar number of migrants this year, and now the situation is so bad that last week Donald Tusk, the president of the European Council – appealed to the world: 'Do not come to Europe.' Too late. [...] Europe truly is on a suicide mission. All we have to decide is whether we want to be part of it ('The EU under siege,' *The Spectator*, 12 March 2016).

A third and strictly related dyad was EU bureaucracy-borders. In fact, Brussels' bureaucrats and bankers were viewed, via a 'top-down' approach which defines Brussels as the vertex imposing 'unnatural' burdens upon historical English liberties and constitutional freedoms or upon British economy (see 'B for Brexit,' *The Economist*, 23 April 2016; 'Between the Borders,' *The Economist*, 18 June 2016).

These discourse topics might be considered – applying Krzyżanowski's language (2016) – as the context of themes that gives rise to further discourses/interdiscursivity matrix at the top of the hierarchy of discourses established by the process of recontextualisation. Although at first sight the findings of this research seem to confirm the assumption that the Eurosceptic press in mis-communicating the complexities of migration promotes an over-simplistic interpretation of Brexit as xenophobia, on the contrary an in-depth context analysis of the editorials and comments reveals a more multifaceted field. Of key interest is how the discourse deployed in the *Remain* press has covered the 'question of European immigrants': across the most committed pro-Remain comments and editorials, immigration was treated in a consolatory way and, in a context where the perception of the EU is aggravated by low levels of awareness of its institutions and policies, this apologetic attitude de facto contributed to 'batting for the other team' (see Fox, 2016; 'The EU is a troubled institution, but we should still vote to remain,' *New Statesman*, 17 June 2016; 'The Sleep of Union,' *The Economist*, 18 June 2016).

Furthermore, both discourses on immigration – the contrite pro-In press and the vocal Brexiteer newspapers – found the same common ground in the topic of the Brussel's governing structure. The entire British press and media system had long been critical, and on more than one occasion with sound arguments, of the EU governance and its bureaucratic nature. The main difference between pro- and anti-EU press has been indicated more in the diverse shades of Euroscepticism, pointing out a distinction between 'hard' and 'soft' tendencies rather than on a clear comparison between different political and ideological positions (Taggart & Szczerbiak, 2008). Hence, arguments such as the EU's democratic 'gap' undermining Westminster institutions, or English liberties and British way of life, or the British political tradition had resonated within the national discourse on Europe for decades, though with varying degrees of emphasis. The aforementioned process of historically defining the European discourse acted therefore as an *operationalising concept*, indeed aiming at operationalising the wider ideological frame of the recontextualization process:

Example 3

One, England has always had a very big sense of sovereignty – we are Britain and are doing this. Two, freedom is very important to England. You have an older tradition than countries like Germany which didn't exist before 1871 and has only been a democracy since 1945 ('I've seen the Future – and it's beautiful,' *The Spectator*, 18 June 2016).

All across the UK, people have seen how we have lost control over so many areas of key national importance. Whether it is our trade, our borders, or who actually makes laws, voters recognise that we have lost the power to make decisions on any of these matters ourselves, and that there is no way to get this back unless we vote to leave (Elliott, 2016).

The second stage of my research investigates how these topics of discourse were repositioned and reordered in the construction of the Brexit discourse (see Figure 1). Or, following Bernstein's terminology, how these topics discursively constructed a new matrix of concepts that have become new *signifiers* (quoted in Krzyżanowski, 2016, p. 317). The first step of the process of recontextualisation engaged with the context of production as well as its decontextualisation (Bernstein, 1990); in the second phase, by combining discourse analysis with history, I intend to further trace the conceptual logic beyond its initial production.

In terms of interdiscursivity, each topos (immigration, economy, EU bureaucracy, and borders) came to the fore framed by a more clear-cut catchphrase which was constantly reconceptualised leaving behind in the process complexity and perspective. Moreover,

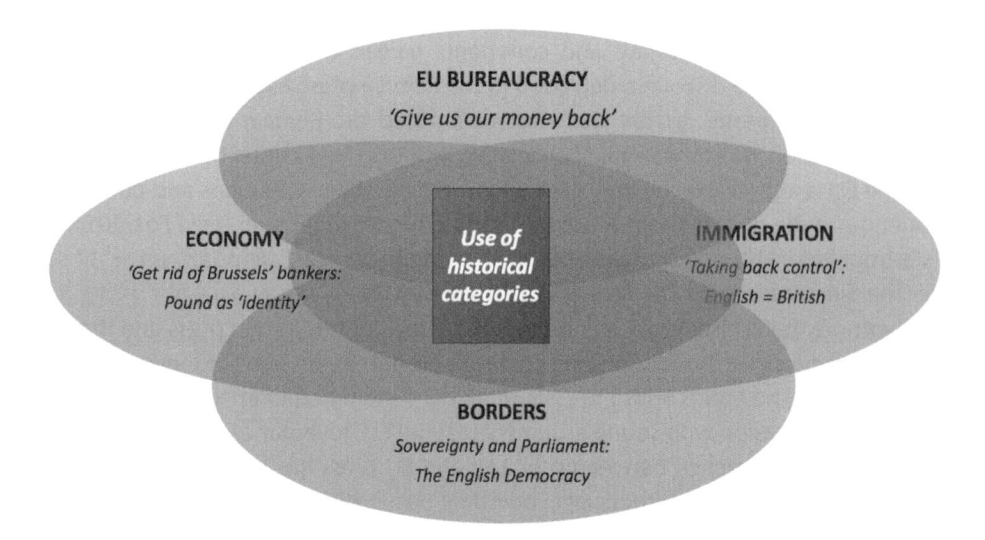

Figure 1. The discursive construction of Brexit: map of interdiscursivity.

each topos was also capable of building discursive relationships with *sister-* and *counter-concepts* (Koselleck, 1988). The selective reproduction of meaning 'translated' the central topics of the discourse into a new matrix of interchangeable concepts, where each of them can be at the same time discursively linked with immigration and economy, or EU bureaucracy or the issue of borders (see Figure 1). They seemed to 'sit comfortably' – to use here Krzyżanowski's language (2016, p. 318) – with each other within the new Brexit framing to the point, as already mentioned, that it is difficult to find structural differences between the pro-In press and the Leave media. For example, the concept of 'taking back control' or the variant 'getting rid of Brussels' bankers' – depending on whether to put more emphasis on the economy or immigration – can also be associated with the supposed EU oligarchy and the necessity to reintroduce 'borders':

Example 4

When the Roman Empire in the West collapsed in the 5th century AD, the invaders' Germanic law took hold (though not over church law). But in the 11th century, bologna University and then others in Italy started using the *Digest* to teach legal reasoning. As a result, Roman law, adapted to the new age, slowly returned over most of Europe. In the 12th century, one Vacarius came to England, where common law reigned, with this exciting new Euro-doctrine. It did not last. In 1234, Henry III banished it for good, and our local common law developed into a body of national law, the first in Europe. The EU ended that independence ('Henry III vs EU law,' *The Spectator*, 30 April 2016).

The EU is undemocratic and run in the interests of business. But it's our least-worst option right now (Laurie Penny fighting words,' *New Statesman*, 10 June 2016).

At the same time, by referring to 'borders' emphasised not only the action of 'taking back control' from a 'corrupt' (*The Daily Telegraph*, 24 June 2016), 'failing' (*The Guardian*, 6 March 2016), 'alien' (*The Times*, 22 May 2016), 'oppressive' (*The Times*, 21 June 2016) and 'anti-democratic' Brussels (*The Spectator*, 18 June 2016), but specularly was reminescent, on the one hand, of the historical category of 'British exceptionalism', which is based upon the Westminster model (primarily understood as 'sovereignty' and 'Parliament'). On the other, it also insisted on the historical concept of 'splendid isolation.' Crucially, within the process of recontextualisation, the UK Pound was used as a by-word for national identity (*The Economist*, 18 June 2016).

The glue that binds together discourses and concepts was thus the reconceptualisation of historical categories. From the nostalgic comments of the *Telegraph* and *Spectator* to the rationalistic pro-EU City-centred editorials of the *Financial Times* or London-centred comments of the *Guardian*, the Brexit discourses developed in the press during the referendum campaign applied 'History as Ideology' (Müller, 2014; Stråth, 2006). According to Hawkins (2012), the main narrative upon which recent British Euroscepticism has been constructed is the 'British exceptionalism' in contrast to the other continental European 'nationalisms' which are more tied up with each other's; whilst Vines (2014) prefers to use the category of 'British political tradition.' Evidence unveiled by this research confirms these interpretations. Another historical category cited was, clearly, the proud efforts of the Second World War. Both fronts, for instance, used the iconic image of Winston Churchill to support their positions on the EU.

This longstanding discourse played a central role within the field of the *Leave* press; remarkably the same argument can be applied to the *Remain* newspapers and on-line journalism.

Both fronts stressed the discursive power of British exceptionalism and the legacy of the splendid isolation, whose continuity with the topic of borders is pivotal: they were of course material borders for the *leavers* and intellectuals or historical borders for the *remainers* with 'English democracy' at stake: a democracy that had to be restored outside Europe for the formers or a system that had to be reinvented inside Europe for the latter.

Discussion and conclusion

According to the journalist-turned-historian Hugo Young, writing about Britain and Europe is writing of a struggle between an unforgettable past and an unavoidable future (Young, 1998, p. 1). The analysis of the editorials and comments during the 2016 European referendum highlights a process of recontextualisation of the discourse of material and immaterial borders between Britain and Europe. The discursive construction of the Britain-Europe dyad emerging from my analysis consists of a confrontation between a new sense of confidence in the country's potential and the pursuit of a new international role for Britain as a champion of free-trade, on the one hand, and the fear of an incumbent economic recession propagandised as the main argument to remain in the EU, on the other. The *Leave* as well as the *Remain* arguments revolved around the 'exceptionalism' of the British political tradition, which supported both the need to leave the EU and 'taking back control' as well as 'keeping the ties' with the continent and reforming the European project. Within this process, an instrumental role to frame the Brexit discourse has been played by the consistent use of historical discourses and concepts.

The analyses of the vote hitherto elaborated have looked for short to middle *durée* political and sociological explanations, mainly putting forward three paradigms: firstly, the Brexit vote as a revolt against the élite and the mainstream austerity narratives and policies. Following this framework, therefore, the result of the referendum vote represented a straightforward rejection of globalisation (Outhwaite, 2017). The conflict between the so-called baby-boomer generation and subsequent generations is a further major sociological rationalisation of the vote of June 2016 (Henderson, Jeffery, Wincott, & Wyn Jones, 2017). Finally, if we accept that Brexit has been misnamed – it was England that voted to leave the EU, not all of the United Kingdom; and the adjective Brexit in front of the substantive discourse could have been easily replaced with 'Engixt' –Brexit might this be interpreted as an expression of English 'populism' and neo-nationalism, which came hard on the heels of a decades-long decline in British national identity. According with this scheme, Brexit discourse finds its roots in the England of vanished industry in the North, rural relative poverty in the Southwest and lower-middle classes in the suburbs of once-great cities. This puzzle took on a 'populist' character: Brexit is a manifestly discourse against multiculturalism and for English neo-nationalism. It is grounded in nostalgia and plays on an old idea of sovereignty (Calhoun, 2017).

This research, on the contrary, advances a new interpretational framework for the Brexit question and discourse: the rise of the 'Anglosphere.' The roots of the Anglosphere concept lie in nineteenth century Imperialist discourses, and more specifically in the idea of an Imperial Federation, which gained ground in the late nineteenth and early twentieth century as the British Empire came under pressure from rising nationalist and anti-colonialist forces (Kenny & Pearce, 2018). The notion of the Anglosphere returned as a central concept in the British political culture in the 1980s and gained momentum amid the Tory's political culture during the New Labour's era as an alternative to the European Union: Anglosphere's potency as a geo-political organising ideal in contrast to the lack of a united or common European foreign policy (Bennett, 2004). Adopted by the Eurosceptic Right-wing as an alternative to the European integration vision, its geo-political claims might have met with some derision in certain political circles and among IR scholars (Gamble, 2003; Wellings & Baxendale, 2015), but the Anglosphere's potency is principally ideological, not geo-political. According to Kenny and Pearce (2016), 'the Anglosphere functions is an imaginary horizon for Britishness,' and places an enormous and contradictory emphasis on the English aspect of Britishness. This notion registers nostalgia, but also energy: what gives it a modern-day appeal is that it frames an account of how an independent UK can prosper in a global economy. Moreover, according to Kenny and Pearce (2016), the pathos of the Anglosphere lies in the idea that Britain will be liberated to march on the world stage again, freed from sclerotic, conformist Europe and reinvigorated by the positive spirits that once gave it an Empire.

Crucially, from the perspective of the Brexit discourse as reconceptualised during the referendum campaign, the Anglo-sphere evokes a way of articulating the national narrative and the identity discourse and, at the same time, it is a way of understanding Britain's place in the world through a new nationalistic sentiment interrelated with the past. The emerging Anglosphere dimension of British political discourse crystallized and reinforced the centrality of national narratives based on a historical interpretation set in opposition to European integration and the European political project. Even the legacy of the Empire, within this recontextualisation of the past, seems to be freed of any sort of responsibility or sense of guilt: a kind of a-historical idea of the British Empire (see Kenny & Pearce, 2018; also Tharoor, 2017; Younge, 2018).

In one of his last articles, the historian Hugh Seaton-Watson (1958) indicated the reason for the British reluctance to accept their 'dual identity' (i.e. British and European) in 'the prevalence in a large part of the British cultural élite of a hangover from Empire in the form of a guilt-complex towards the peoples of Asia and Africa.' It seems that now, within the Brexit discourse, the sense of guilt associated with the Imperial cultural legacy described by Seton-Watson has disappeared and, instead of a sincere appropriation of the dual identity, this new historical notion of the British Empire is mainly linked with only positive aspects of the British political tradition such as the principles of free trade, the rule of law or the parliamentary democracy. This traditional narrative is part of a re-engagement with 'traditional allies' within the Anglosphere aiming at answering a dilemma about Britain's future framed in terms of an English traditional reading of the past (Wellings, 2016). As a result, within the Brexit discourse historical arguments and historical categories have played a focal role, not only representing the point of departure but concluding its parabola as the place of destination.

Notes

1. Among the daily newspapers the biggest winners were the *Guardian* (with circulation up by 3.63%) and *The Times* (up 2.51%). Johnston Press's *I* rose 2.97%, the pro-Brexit *The Telegraph* a more modest 1.12% while the *Daily Mail* could only muster a 0.28% rise (Sweney, 2016).
2. The term describes the foreign policy pursued by Britain during the late nineteenth century under the Conservative Party's premierships of Benjamin Disraeli and Lord Salisbury.

Disclosure statement

No potential conflict of interest was reported by the author.

References

Albertazzi, D., & McDonnel, D. (2015). *Populist in power*. Houndmills: Routledge.

Balch, A., & Balabanova, E. (2016). Ethics, politics and migration: Public debates on the free movement of Romanians and Bulgarians in the UK, 2006–2013. *Politics, 36*(1), 19–35.

Balch, A., & Balabanova, E. (2017). A deadly cocktail? The fusion of Europe and immigration in the UK press. *Critical Discourse Studies, 14*(3), 236–255.

Bell, D. (2007). *The idea of Greater Britain. Empire and the future of world order, 1860–1900*. Princeton: Princeton University Press.

Bennett, J. (2004). *The anglosphere challenge: Why the English-speaking nations will lead the way in the twenty first century*. Lanham, MD: Rowman & Littlefield.

Bernstein, B. (1990). *Class, codes and control, Vol. IV: The structuring of pedagogic discourse*. London: Routledge.

Berry, M. (2016). Understanding the role of the mass media in the EU referendum. In D. Jackson, E. Thorsen, & D. Wring (Eds.), *EU referendum analysis 2016: Media, voters and the campaign* (p. 14). Poole: The Centre for the Study of Journalism, Culture and Community, Bournemouth University.

Blagden, D. (2017). Britain and the world after Brexit. *International Politics, 54*(1), 1–25.

Bogdanor, V. (2005). Footfalls echoing in the memory. Britain and Europe: The historical perspective. *International Affairs, 81*(4), 689–701.

Bourdieu, P. (1993 [1983]). *The field of cultural production*. Cambridge: Polity Press.

Calhoun, C. (2017). Populism, nationalism and Brexit. In W. Outhwaite (Ed.), *Brexit. Sociological response* (pp. 57–76). London: Anthem Press.

Clarke, H. D., Goodwin, M., & Whiteley, P. (2017). *Brexit. Why Britain voted to leave the European Union*. Cambridge: Cambridge University Press.

Daddow, O. (2004). *Britain and Europe since 1945: Historiographical Perspectives on integration*. Manchester: Manchester University Press.

Daddow, O. (2006). Euroscepticism and history education in Britain. *Government and Opposition, 41* (1), 64–85.

Daddow, O. (2013). *New labour and the European Union: Blair and Brown's logic of history*. Oxford: Oxford University Press.

Diamond, P., Nedergaard, P., & Rosamond, B. (2018). *The Routledge handbook of politics of Brexit*. Houndmills: Routledge.

Eaton, G. (2016, June 24). Why neither side could tell the truth about immigration in the EU referendum campaign. *New Statesman*.

Elliott, M. (2016, March 8). Why Britain will choose the safer option and vote leave. *opendemocracy.net*.

Fairclough, N., & Wodak, R. (1997). Critical discourse analysis. In T. A. Van Dijk (Ed.), *Discourses & society* (pp. 811–819). London: SAGE.

Firmstone, J. (2016). Newspapers' editorial Opinions during the referendum campaign. In D. Jackson, E. Thorsen, & D. Wring (Eds.), *EU referendum analysis 2016: Media, voters and the campaign* (p. 36). Poole: The Centre for the Study of Journalism, Culture and Community, Bournemouth University.

Fox, J. (2016, April 4). Britain and the EU: A gulf in understanding. *opendemocracy.net*.

Freeden, M. (2017). After the Brexit referendum: Revisiting populism as an ideology. *Journal of Political Ideologies, 22*(1), 1–11.

Gamble, A. (2003). *Between Europe and America: The future of British politics*. Basingstoke: Palgrave.

Greenslade, R. (2004). *Press gang: How newspapers make profits from propaganda*. London: Macmillan.

Grob-Fitzgibbon, B. (2016). *Continental drift. Britain and Europe from the end of empire to the rise of Euroscepticism*. Cambridge: Cambridge University Press.

Hall, I. (2012). *Dilemmas of decline. British intellectuals and the world politics, 1945–1975*. Berkeley: University of California Press.

Harrison, B. (2009). *Seeking a role. The United Kingdom 1951–1970*. Oxford: Oxford University Press.

Harvey, D. (2005). *A brief history of neoliberalism*. Oxford: Oxford University Press.

Hawkins, B. (2012). Nation, separation and threat: An analysis of British media discourses on the European Union treaty reform process. *JCMS: Journal of Common Market Studies, 50*(4), 561–577.

Henderson, A., Jeffery, C., Wincott, D., & Wyn Jones, R. (2017). How Brexit was made in England. *The British Journal of Politics and International Relations, 19*(4), 631–646.

Hopkin, P. (2017). When Polanyi met farage: Market fundamentalism, economic nationalisation, and Britain's Exit from the European Union. *The British Journal of Politics and International Relations, 19* (3), 465–478.

Inglehart, R. F., & Norris, P. (2016). *Trump, Brexit, and the rise of populism: Economic have-nots and cultural backlash*. Cambridge, MA: Faculty Research Working Papers, Harvard Kennedy School.

Jackson, D., Thorsen, E., & Wring, D. (Eds.). (2016). *EU referendum analysis 2016: Media, voters and the campaign*. Poole: The Centre for the Study of Journalism, Culture and Community, Bournemouth University.

Kenny, M., & Pearce, N. (2016). After Brexit: The Eurosceptic dream of an anglosphere. *Juncture, 22*(4), 304–307.

Kenny, M., & Pearce, N. (2018). *Shadows of Empire: The anglosphere in British politics*. London: Polity.

Koselleck, R. (1988). *Critique and crisis: Enlightenment and the pathogenesis of modern society*. Oxford: Berg.

Krzyżanowski, M. (2010). *The discursive construction of European identities*. Frankfurt am Main: Peter Lang.

Krzyżanowski, M. (2013). Discourses and concepts: Interfaces and synergies between *Begriffsgeschichte* and the discourse-historical approach in CDA. In R. Wodak (Ed.), *Critical discourse analysis* (Vol. 4, pp. 201–214). London: SAGE.

Krzyżanowski, M. (2016). Recontextualization of neoliberalism and the increasingly conceptual nature of discourse: Challenges for critical discourse studies. *Discourse & Society, 27*(3), 308–321.

Levy, D. A. L., Aslan, B., & Bironzo, D. (Eds.). (2016). *UK press coverage of the EU referendum*. Oxford: Reuters Institute for the Study of Journalism, University of Oxford.

Maccaferri, M. (2009). A splenetic isolation. Dibattito pubblico e intellettuali inglesi di fronte all'Affair Suez. *Ventunesimo Secolo, 9*(2), 109–126.

Maccaferri, M. (2017). British intellectuals and the European idea after the Suez crisis. Narrating Europe between history and politics. *Journal of British Identities, 1*(1), 1–13.

Marquand, D. (2008). *Britain since 1918. The strange career of British democracy*. London: Weidenfeld & Nicolson.

Moffitt, B. (2016). *The global rise of populism. Performance, political style, and representation*. Stanford: Stanford University Press.

Müller, J.-W. (2014). On conceptual history. In D. M. McMahon & S. Moyn (Eds.), *Rethinking modern European intellectual history* (pp. 74–93). Oxford: Oxford University Press.

Müller, J.-W. (2016). *What is populism?* Philadelphia: University of Pennsylvania Press.

Nairn, T. (1977). *The break-up of Britain: Crisis and neo-nationalism*. London: New Left Books.

Outhwaite, W. (2017). *Brexit. Sociological response*. London: Anthem Press.

Parry, J. (2006). *The politics of patriotism. English liberalism, national identity and Europe, 1830–1886*. Cambridge: Cambridge University Press.

Schulz-Forberg, H., & Olsen, N. (2014). Actors and network in transnational and national spaces: Towards a new history of liberalism in Europe. In H. Schulz-Forberg & N. Olsen (Eds.), *Re-inventing western civilisation* (pp. 1–10). Newcastle upon Tyne: Cambridge Scholars Publishing.

Seaton-Watson, H. (1958, July–August). What is Europe, where is Europe? From mystique to politique. *Encounter*, p. 15.

Stråth, B. (2006). Ideology and history. *Journal of Political Ideologies, 11*(1), 23–42.

Stråth, B., & Wodak, R. (2009). Europe – discourse – politics – media – history: Constructing "crises". In A. Triandafyllidou, R. Wodak, & M. Krzyżanowski (Eds.), *The European public sphere and the media* (pp. 15–33). Basingstoke: Macmillan.

Sweney, M. (2016, July 21). Brexit vote boosts national newspaper sales. *The Guardian*.

Taggart, P., & Szczerbiak, A. (Eds.). (2008). *Opposing Europe?: The comparative party politics of Euroscepticism: Volume 1 and Volume 2*. Oxford: Oxford University Press.

Tharoor, I. (2017, March 31). Brexit and Britain's delusions of empire. *The Washington Post*.

Tomlinson, J. (2009). Thrice denied: "declinism" as a recurrent theme in British history in the long twentieth century. *Twentieth Century British History, 20*(2), 227–251.

Varouxakis, G. (2010). Mid-Atlantinc musings: The "question of Europe" in British intellectual debates 1961–2008. In J. Lacroix & K. Nicoladïs (Eds.), *European stories. Intellectual debates on Europe in national contexts* (pp. 147–166). Oxford: Oxford University Press.

Vines, E. (2014). Reframing English nationalism and Euroscepticism: From populism to the British political tradition. *British Politics, 9*(3), 255–274.

Wellings, B. (2016). *Our Island Story*: England, Europe and the anglosphere alternative. *Political Studies Review, 14*(3), 368–377.

Wellings, B., & Baxendale, H. (2015). Euroscepticism and the anglosphere: Traditions and dilemmas in contemporary English nationalism. *JCMS: Journal of Common Market Studies, 53*(1), 123–139.

Westlake, M. (2017). The increasing inevitability of *that* referendum. In W. Outhwaite (Ed.), *Brexit. Sociological response* (pp. 3–170). London: Anthem Press.

Wilson, G. (2017). Brexit, Trump and the special relationship. *The British Journal of Politics and International Relations, 19*(3), 543–557.

Wincott, D. (2017). Brexit dilemmas: New opportunities and tough choices in unsettled times. *The British Journal of Politics and International Relations, 19*(4), 680–695.

Wincott, D., Peterson, J., & Convey, A. (2017). Introduction: Studying Brexit's causes and consequences. *The British Journal of Politics and International Relations, 19*(3), 429–433.

Wodak, R., & Meyer, M. (Eds.). (2009). *Methods of critical discourse analysis*. London: Sage.

Wright, T., & Gamble, A. (2000). Commentary: The end of Britain? *The Political Quarterly, 71*(1), 1–3.

Young, H. (1998). *This blessed plot. Britain and Europe from Churchill to Blair*. London: Macmillan.

Younge, G. (2018, February 3). Britain's imperial fantasies have given us Brexit. *Financial Times*.

The Brexit referendum: how trade and immigration in the discourses of the official campaigns have legitimised a toxic (inter)national logic

Franco Zappettini ⓘ

ABSTRACT

This paper analyses the discourses produced on their websites by the two organisations that conducted the official 'leave' and 'remain' campaigns in the Brexit referendum. The analysis, which adopts the general orientation of the Discourse Historical Approach in CDS, is aimed at illuminating the main discursive strategies, argumentative schemes and key representations of Britain in/and Europe that sustained the ideological (de)legitimation of Brexit on either side. Based on this analysis, this paper argues that the specific ideological articulation of two key discursive elements – namely trade and immigration – and the argumentative schemes deployed in the campaign engendered and legitimised a new toxic (inter)national logic of Brexit: by leaving the EU, Britain 'takes back control' to pursue mercantile policies whose benefits 'outsiders' should be excluded from.

1. Introduction

The UK's choice to leave EU constitutes an unprecedented political event which is likely to have profound repercussions on British and European societies for years to come. Why and how it happened, as well as its current and future impact have been the concern of an extensive body of academic work and no doubt these questions will carry on being debated for some time.

This paper contributes to this general debate by approaching Brexit as the historic conjuncture of different social and discursive trajectories (see Zappettini and Krzyzanowski, 2019) and by focusing on the process of their institutional legitimisation. In particular, taking the vantage point of the referendum debate and its mediatisation, this paper analyses the discourses (re)produced and circulated on the websites of the two organisations designated by the UK Electoral Commission as the official lead campaigns for the 'leave' and 'remain' vote. These were, respectively, Vote Leave (VL) and Britain Stronger In Europe (BSE) (henceforth only referred to by their acronyms).

The reason for focusing on these organisations is that VL and BSE were key semi-institutional actors in the process of legitimisation of Brexit effectively contributing to setting the referendum agenda. Both organisations were backed up by business groups and other vested interests and had cross-party political support (as further elaborated below); becoming the lead campaign allowed them to access vital public resources[1] and to give significant exposure to their messages in the public domain whilst escalating certain political and social demands up the institutional chain of discourses (Fairclough, 2003). From this prominent standpoint, therefore, VL and BSE had the power to influence public opinion on the meaning of Brexit and to frame the context of the debate by reproducing, challenging or silencing certain discourses and ideologies which they were able to associate with the generic binaries 'leave' and 'remain'.

Trading on these premises, the aim of this paper is to investigate which messages the two leading campaigns fostered in the public domain to support the desired outcome of the referendum vote and how such messages contributed to the wider conjuncture of Brexit. In particular, this paper delves into the main discursive strategies, argumentative schemes and key representations of Britain in/and Europe that sustained the (de)legitimation of Brexit on either side to address the fundamental questions: 'why and how did Brexit occur and for whose benefit'? It is contended that, through the institutional framing of the referendum campaign in antagonistic camps, the ideological articulation of discourses of trade and immigration engendered and legitimised a new toxic (inter)national logic of Brexit: by leaving the EU, Britain 'takes back control' to pursue mercantile policies whose benefits 'outsiders' should be excluded from.

This paper adopts the general theoretical and methodological orientation of the Discourse Historical Approach (DHA) (Krzyżanowski, 2010; Wodak, 2009). Drawing on the DHA heuristic operationalisation Section two discusses the socio-political background, the specific institutional framing, and the genre of the Brexit referendum campaign. Section three unpacks the analytical approach applied to the data. Section four presents and discusses the most salient findings and some critical conclusions are finally drawn in Section five.

2. The context of production of discourses

2.1. Social and political background to the Brexit referendum

Since joining the then EEC in 1973, British Governments have historically adopted an 'outsider' stance towards the European project (Daddow, 2015) regarding it primarily as a transactional affair rather than a political goal or a social endeavour. Following the expansion of the EU over the last two decades, British Euroscepticism and opposition to European integration have increasingly been appropriated by domestic politics defining the resurgence of English nationalism (Wellings, 2007). Notably, in the last few years, the UK's discomfort with EU-rope have coincided with the rise of the right-wing UK Independence Party (UKIP). Fuelled by UKIP's propaganda and widely echoed by the strongly anti-EU tabloid press, calls for an 'independent' Britain and for a 'repatriation' of powers from Brussels became increasingly widespread discourses among Tory 'rebel' backbenchers. In response to these demands, in 2013 the then Prime Minister David Cameron pledged that the next Conservative government would ask the British people for a mandate to negotiate a new settlement with the EU. Having won the general elections in 2015 and having reached a 'deal' with his EU partners, Mr Cameron called for an in/out referendum whilst he pledged to champion the UK's continuing membership of the EU.

Significantly, the referendum took place amid a series of economic and humanitarian 'crises' and in the eighth year of austerity politics that had exacerbated social inequalities in European and British societies. As Jessop (2017) notes:

> The crucial issue that remained largely unvoiced [in Brexit] was that real or imagined crisis symptoms were not caused by membership of the European Union as such. Rather, they were rooted in its neoliberal form, the crisis of Eurozone crisis-management, and the long-run failure to address crucial domestic issues that undermined economic and extra-economic competitiveness. (p. 138)

In many respects, the referendum stirred the public sentiment over the causes of this economic crisis and became to be regarded by many as a symbolic vote about economic issues, globalisation, and multiculturalism as much as it was about the UK-EU relationship. As post-referendum research into socio-demographics has shown, the UK regions that voted for Brexit were also those areas most affected by growing social, cultural, and economic inequalities (Savage and Cunningham, 2016). The Brexit vote however also played out along several other axes showing that several dividing lines and cleavages existed within the British voters based on their age, education, urban vs. rural locations and their attitudes towards open/close views of the world (Cooper, 2016).

According to a poll conducted in February 2016 (Kellner, 2016) there was a distinct divide between 'leavers' and 'remainers' in where the two sides believed the causes of the UK's economic problems lay. For 'in' voters, the top three factors to blame were British banks, the Conservative-led government since 2010 and growing inequality. For 'out' voters these were: EU rules and regulations, immigrants willing to work for low wages and the last Labour government. In other words, for 'leavers' the causes of the crisis were factors outside the UK, while for 'remainers' the factors were internal to the UK. Similarly, according to another poll (Bailey, 2016) immigration topped the list of the most important issues in the EU referendum for 'leavers' but was much less important for 'remainers'. Crucially, the concern with immigration became particularly acute in the two weeks before the referendum when '[i]mmigration ha[d] now surpassed the economy becoming the most important issue for voters' (Skinner, 2016). According to the same survey, by focusing on immigration issues, the leave campaign was getting better traction, for example with 45 per cent of the sample of voters believing that a vote for remain would be followed by Turkey gaining fast-track entry to the EU and its population effectively granted free movement into the UK. These negative perceptions were compounded (and amplified by the media, especially British tabloids) in public discourses of 'Europe in crisis' which followed the series of terrorist attacks in various European cities and the displacement of Syrian and other refugees who had attempted to reach Europe. These different representations of crisis contributed to create general negative perceptions of European freedom of movement and to frame immigration flows as a threat to Britain.

Finally, domestic political factors must also be considered as the context in which discourses of the referendum played out. Firstly, the Conservative party saw a number of cabinet members breaking ranks to join the 'leave' campaign as they were in disagreement with the PM whom they accused of having brought home from Brussels an unsatisfactory and too watered down 'deal'. Whilst the remain campaign was notably supported by the PM and the Chancellor of Exchequer, the leave campaign was championed by key figures such as Michael Gove and Boris Johnson who were instrumental in mass mediating the 'leave' message. Secondly, the Labour Party failed to commit to a convincing unified stance with its leader Jeremy Corbyn – who had previously declared himself a Eurosceptic – only showing a lukewarm support for the 'remain' choice towards the later stages of the campaign.

2.2. Institutional framing and actors of the Brexit campaign

Along with the macro socio-political context, one must also consider the institutional framing of the debate as a key context in which discourse of Brexit emerged and were circulated during the campaign. As Koopmans and Olzak (2004) suggest in relation to political mobilisation, the political-institutional setting in which discourses are embedded provides 'discursive opportunities' (and constraints) for the framing, diffusion, and impact of messages in the public sphere. Visibility, resonance, and public legitimacy of discourse are acquired (or challenged) through the interaction of key actors along the discursive chain: the claim makers, the institutional gatekeepers, and the media (Fairclough, 2003).

In the case of Brexit, the call for the referendum polarised different interests and different actors around pro-Remain/Leave programmes which competed to be designated as the official lead campaigns by the Electoral Commission. The Electoral Commission is an independent body set up by the UK Parliament which regulates party and election finance and sets standards for well-run elections. As, in the case of referendums, its task is to choose the candidate whom 'represent those campaigning for the [referendum] outcome to the greatest extent' (Electoral Commission, 2016), the Electoral Commission effectively acted as a key institutional gatekeeper of the debate framing.

On 13 April 2016 the Electoral Commission designated VL and BSE as the official campaign on each side. BSE was a Westminster-based group backed by different pro-EU campaign associations and relied on funding from different financial organisations and businesspersons. VL branched out of Business for Britain, a coalition of Eurosceptics linked to the Confederation of British Industry, and was backed by senior Conservative as well as Labour politicians. Each organisation was, in turn, endorsed by civic and business associations.[2] Whilst BSE was the only applicant for the Remain side, the GO movement – notably supported by UKIP's Nigel Farage and funded by multi-millionaire donor Arron Banks – was the other major 'leave' contender. Despite some initial in-fights between VL and the GO movement following the Electoral Commission's decision, Nigel Farage claimed that his party 'would work with anyone who wanted to leave the EU' (The Independent, 2016). Similarly, UKIP's donor Mr Banks expressed his support for VL as he saw its appointment as conveniently appealing to those Eurosceptics who regarded Mr. Farage as a too divisive figure (BBC, 2016). Whilst therefore operating from the background, UKIP would effectively run a parallel campaign in support of VL, voicing in particular the 'question of immigration' which shifted the centre of gravity away from the original VL's economic case for leaving the EU.

Crucially, the institutional endorsement of VL and BSE as the two lead campaigns (and the media amplification of their messages) contributed to define the discursive frame of the debate along the particular agendas of the two organisations, allowing them to escalate the political demands of their representatives and to project on the Leave/Remain binaries selected representations of the issues at stake.

2.3. Media entextualisation of Brexit discourses

Texts produced for referendum campaigns belong to a discursive genre aimed at forming public opinion and persuading voters in favour of a particular choice by legitimising a specific political goal or course of action as the 'right' choice (in this case leaving or remaining in the EU). As shown by a range of studies (Vreese, 2007), depending on the issue being deliberated, referendum campaigns can conform to a rational genre of deliberative argumentation (for example drawing on facts to construct arguments) as well as to a genre that mainly appeals to emotional and ideological positions (such as the sense of belonging to national or political communities). With Internet-based platforms increasingly appropriated in politics as powerful machineries in the strategic mobilisation of public opinion (Chadwick & Howard, 2010) these discursive genres have gradually moved towards digitalised productions. In the case of the Brexit referendum, the digital mediatisation of messages was instrumental to the final outcome of the referendum as a large proportion of the advertising budget of the lead campaigns was spent online and involved delivering the key messages to undecided voters via 'big data' aggregation and social media targeting (Hilder, 2017).

The process of digital entextualisation of the campaign thus opened up new 'discursive opportunities' for the key referendum actors to de/recontextualise historical and ongoing discourses of Britain and/in Europe into new semiotic realisations that would fit into or indeed drive the leave/remain narratives. Crucially, in the process of entextualisation new interdiscursive relations between arguments and other linguistic elements could potentially be created which would create new orders of discourses and enable new logics associated with them to be (re)produced (Krzyżanowski, 2016).

3. Data and analytical approach

Data was derived from the official websites of the two organisations.[3] Websites were consulted regularly between October 2015 and the end of June 2016 as this time frame effectively represents the period of maximum activity. This preliminary survey showed that both websites presented fairly similar features including the following prominent sections which discussed 'facts' about the EU and Britain and in which the case was made for either leaving or remaining: 'Why vote leave?' and 'Facts about the European Union'(VL) and 'The basics' and 'FAQs' (BSE).

The analysis focused on the discursive realisations which were directly available on the website pages of each of the above sections or accessible via hypertextual links through these pages. This corpus of data, consisting of a total of 81 pages of texts (which also included pictures and, in the case of VL, cartoons), was analysed at discourse-pragmatic and semiotic levels using the DHA analytical operationalisation (Krzyżanowski, 2010). This consists of: (a) a thematic analysis mapping the key analytical categories or discourse topics and (b) an in-depth or argumentation-oriented analysis involving the investigation of discursive strategies, topoi and their means and forms of realisation. Particular attention was paid to the systematic analysis of argumentative schemes and warrants (Toulmin, 1958) which supported the main claim 'the UK should remain in/leave the EU'. In the tradition of the DHA, the analysis mapped the topoi (or fallacies) which were implicitly or explicitly invoked to justify arguments as, for example, the conditional or causal logics 'if x then y' or 'y because x' (Reisigl, 2014). In synergy with this standard operationalisation of the DHA, the analysis also zeroed in on the use of narratives and specific representations of the world as premises for framing argumentative schemes (Fairclough & Fairclough, 2012). The analysis therefore mapped representations which specifically supported the 'leave/remain' claims following Fairclough and Fairclough's distinction between: (i) circumstantial premises (representing the context of action and identifying the issue to be solved); (ii) goal premises (geared towards the achievement of desirable states of affairs); and (iii) means premises (how to achieve the set goal).

4. Analysis

4.1. Discursive macro-topics and interdiscursive relations

BSE's discourses primarily hinged on representations of the EU as the Single Market and mainly focused on highlighting the benefits of the status quo and the risk of leaving the Single Market. BSE's discourses largely discussed economic topics and, in some cases, also social and political implications derived from the membership of the Single Market (e.g. workers' rights). In addition to the dominant economic framing, BSE's discursive topics included international relations and relied on representations of Britain as an actor in different systems of power. Whilst VL also engaged with topics related with the economy, its discourses were clearly framed within a neoliberal dimension and were driven in particular by representations of the constraints of the EU rules and EU laws on British businesses and on British aspirations to wider global trade. Notably, whilst early discourses of VL discussed economic topics and the question of sovereignty via legal and political arguments (discursively linked with Eurosceptic narratives), towards the final weeks of the campaign the focus of the Leave campaign increasingly shifted towards topics of immigration and free movement (paralleled by the UKIP campaign) as further discussed in the next section. By contrast, topics related to migration and sovereignty were only marginally discussed by BSE. A list of the main discursive topics covered by both organisations and the main interdiscursive relations is provided in Figures 1 and 2 while the main argumentative schemes are discussed in detail in the next section.

4.2. In-depth analysis

4.2.1. Main argumentative schemes of the 'remain' campaign

Discursive strategies of BSE were aimed, on the one hand, at highlighting the current benefits of the EU membership whilst, on the other, at emphasising the negative impact of Brexit on jobs, economic and social prosperity (as summarised in Figure 1

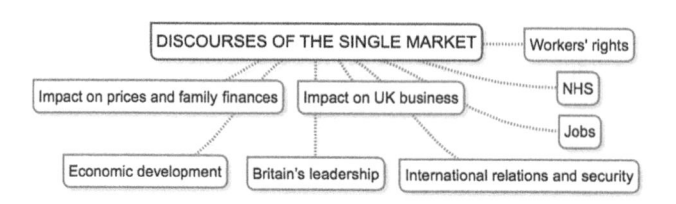

Figure 1. BSE's main discursive topics and main interdiscursive relations.

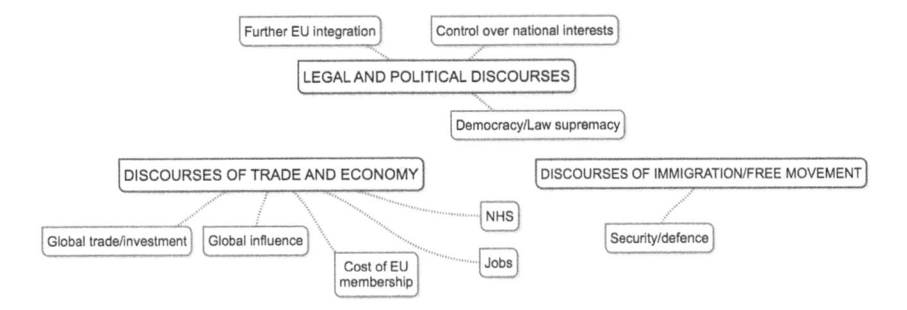

Figure 2. VL's main discursive topics and main interdiscursive relations.

and Table 1). Whilst the former strategy was achieved through positive topoi such as the *topos of benefit*, the latter strategy tended to project a negative scenario for the UK outside the EU (which the leave campaign dubbed 'project fear') and was driven by different *topoi of risk*. Both strategies were characterised by the overt nominalisation of 'you and your family' as the addressee of the benefits and the negative consequences and potential risk. Moreover, another conspicuous pattern in BSE discourses was the frequent reference to some authoritative source (*argumentum ad verecundiam*) to back up the credibility of the warrant and the conclusions as illustrated below:

Extract 1

Over 3 million UK jobs are linked to our trade with the EU: one in every ten jobs in this country (Source: HM Treasury) […] If we leave the EU experts predict that the economic hit would mean up to 950,000 UK jobs could be lost (Source: Confederation of British Industry), meaning less security for you and your family.

Another prominent set of discourses emerging in the Remain campaign related to international relations and security through which BSE represented 'Britain's place in the world'. In this case, BSE made the case for remaining by emphasising Britain's leadership on the international stage through the *topos of (inter)national influence*:

Extract 2

Being a leading member of the EU, as well as in NATO and the UN, ensures that Britain can stand tall in the world and promote our own interests.

In this case, whilst the *topos of (inter)national influence* validates the argument for remaining, it also represents the EU as union of states which must safeguard their own interests rather than an entity with supranational aims. In this sense the argument

Table 1. Summary of BSE main discursive strategies, topoi, and representations.

Main Strategies	Main Topoi/Fallacies	Key Representations
Emphasising the benefits of EU membership Emphasising how Brexit would affect individuals and households Representing Britain's 'place in the world'.	Topos of benefit Topos of risk avoidance Topos of authority Topos of (inter)national influence	Individuals and families as part of an economic system The EU as the Single Market The world as an international system of powers

project an ideal clout that Britain would carry by being in an international 'members' club' (along with the UN and Nato) and the national benefits deriving from such memberships.

Notably, BSE did not engage substantively with discourses of immigration. Its discussion of this topic was limited to marginal representations of British citizens benefitting from visa-free opportunities to study, travel and retire anywhere across the EU and to representations of British businesses being able to benefit from the free movement of labour (Figure 3).

4.2.2. Main argumentative schemes of the 'leave' campaign

The main discursive thrust of the Leave side was the representation of 'independence' from the EU as an essential condition for the UK to be in control of its domestic affairs and to pursue an agenda of (inter)national (neo)liberalism. This macro argumentative scheme (as represented in Figure 2) was supported by the *topos of sovereignty loss* which can be broken down as follows: Britain has lost its sovereignty to the EU (circumstantial premise) which it should regain (goal premise) by no longer being an EU member (means premise). This overarching scheme was reproduced in more specific arguments in three distinct areas: economy, political/legal integration, and immigration which are discussed below and are summarised in Table 2 in relation to main discursive strategies, topoi, and representations (Figure 4).

4.2.3. Economic arguments

VL's early discourses focused on strategies of delegitimation of the EU and were predicated on economic arguments which represented Britain's economic potential as 'constrained', 'tie down' or 'dominated' by the EU. A number of arguments which characterised the leave choice as 'freeing' Britain from an unresponsive and costly EU were based on *topoi of burden* for British businesses and were realised via the expression 'red tape', a euphemism for employment rights and social and environmental protection. Moreover, VL advocated the 'leave' choice through discourses of free trade[4] in which the

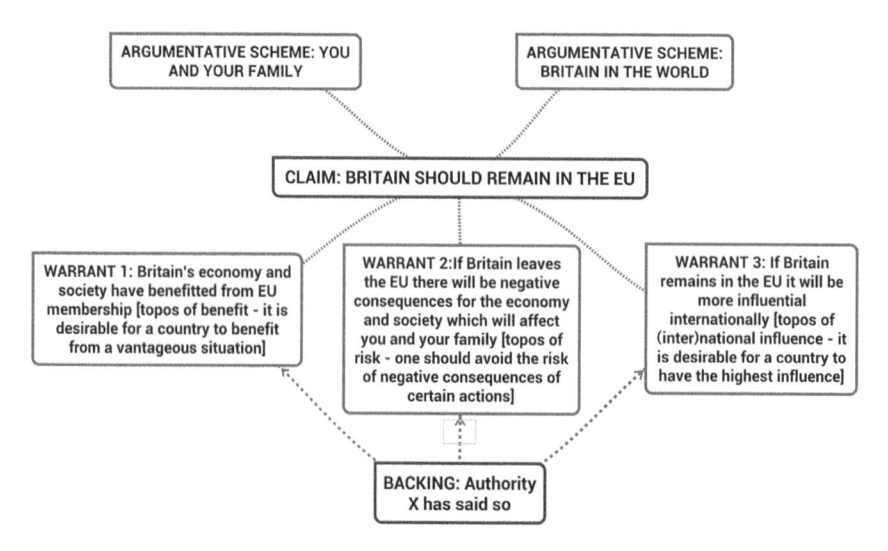

Figure 3. Main argumentative schemes of the Remain campaign.

Table 2. Summary of BSE main discursive strategies, topoi, and representations.

Main Strategies	Main Topoi/Fallacies	Key Representations
Delegitimising the EU Prioritising economic resources	Topos of sovereignty loss over trade Topos of burden for businesses Topos/fallacy of (inter)national influence Topos of pro bono nobis	Britain 'constrained' 'tied down' or 'dominated' by the EU Independent Free trade deals as the solution to globalisation Britain as a 'proud trading nation' National vs. transnational solidarity
Rejecting or resisting political integration	Topos of risk avoidance Topos of EU law supremacy	The UK ostracised by other EU countries and dragged into a closer Union The ECJ meddling with British affairs
Constructing moral panic around immigration	Topos of sovereignty loss (over border control) Topos/fallacy of numbers Fallacy of risk avoidance Fallacy of public safety	Britain at risk of invasion by millions of migrants Conflation of EU freedom of movement and illegal migration Open border' Europe and 'border vulnerability' – Conflation of immigrant and criminals/terrorists

EU was delegitimised as unresponsive and preventing the UK from seizing worldwide economic opportunities. Representations of 'free trade deals' were often discursively embraced as powerful – albeit simplistic – solutions to the constraints of the EU membership and the issue of reduced or lost sovereignty:

Extract 3

Technological and economic forces are changing the world fast. EU institutions cannot cope. We have lost control of vital policies. This is damaging. We need a new relationship. [...] We negotiate a new UK-EU deal based on free trade and friendly cooperation. We end the supremacy of EU law. We regain control.

Extract 4

We regain the power to make our own trade deals with countries around the world. We regain an independent voice in world trade negotiations with independent voting rights at the World Trade Organisation. We regain seats on other international rule-setting bodies that we've given away to the EU. We use our stronger international influence to work for closer international cooperation.

In Extract 4 the argument for leaving is constructed along a simplistic logic of 'cause and solution'. It rests on distinct circumstantial premises that represent globalisation as driven by external and non-agent specific forces and on the representation of the EU as an unfit

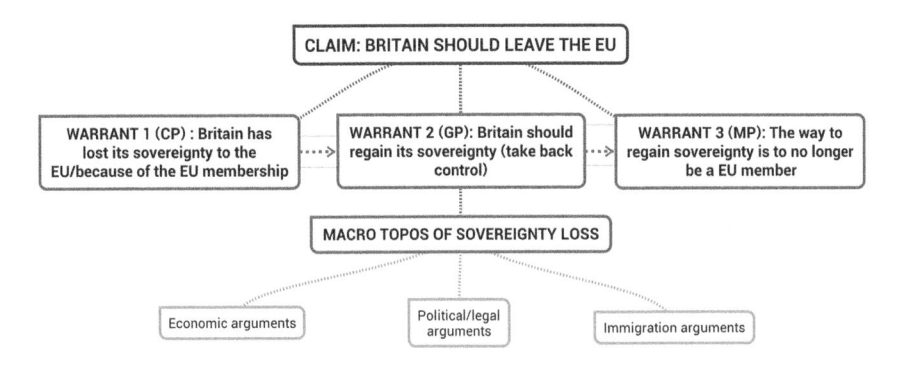

Figure 4. Main argumentative scheme of the Leave campaign.

actor vis-à-vis such forces. The legitimation of voting leave as 'taking control' is achieved via a series of functional moves (implicitly connected albeit missing explicit causative connectives) towards the negotiation of a free trade UK-EU deal which is presented to the reader as the solution to the problem of globalisation. Similarly, the argument put forward in Extract 5 hinges on a representation of the UK 'regaining' the power lost to the EU at the WTO table and it rests on a set of goal premises which legitimise Brexit as a means to a mercantile goal. In this case, the means premise is predicated on the *topos of (inter)national influence* that the UK would be able to fully deploy better than the EU inside the WTO and on the international stage were it an actor of its own rather than being represented by the EU. In this sense, rather than a rationally warranted premise, the *topos of (inter)national influence* appears to be used as a fallacious rhetorical device which appeals to a nostalgic vision of Britain's leadership as a 'proud trading nation' and which leverages on the British aspirations to be recognised again as a great power in its own right (see Zappettini, 2019 for the imaginary of 'global Britain').

Another set of economic arguments legitimising the leave choice relied on strategies of prioritising *us* over *them* (often metonymically associated with Brussels) in the sharing of economic resources and were typically realised through the *topos of pro bono nobis* (for our own benefit). One of the most prominent arguments in this sense was about the 'wasted' money that Britain pays into the EU budget which, VL claimed, should benefit nationals rather than 'outsiders':

Extract 5

We send about £350 million to Brussels every week. […] If we vote to 'remain', it is a vote for the permanent payment to Brussels of all this money. […] All this money could be better spent on the NHS, schools, and fundamental science research. […] If we vote to leave, we can change the agenda. If we regain the power to control our own affairs, we can sort out our own problems

This argument (which captured the public imagination also in virtue of a red bus campaign associated with the slogan 'We send the EU £ 350 million a week. Let's fund our NHS instead') was predicated on a figure which was at best arbitrary as admitted by the leave campaign director.[5] More significantly, the legitimacy of 'taking control' tapped into the symbolic national appeal of education and health systems (both are outside the remit of EU policies; the NHS is the UK's biggest employer and has always represented a sensitive topic in political campaigns).

4.2.4. Political and legal arguments

Arguments which represented voting leave as 'freeing' the UK from increasing political and legal integration with other European countries were also frequent. These arguments largely reproduced the macro argumentative schemes underpinned by the *topos of sovereignty loss* (as discussed earlier) to reject Europe as a political project. In some cases, the leave arguments were also realised through *topoi of risk avoidance* for example in relation to the Euro crisis:

Extract 6

It is not unreasonable to assume that a 'Yes' vote will be taken as a mandate for the UK to one day join the Euro – and effectively sail towards disaster. A 'No' vote at the upcoming referendum on EU membership is the only way to prevent an inevitable slide towards further economic and political integration before it's too late.

In a few other instances, political arguments were mostly driven by the *topos of (inter)-national influence* which represented the EU as an arena of national interests to be defended and Britain's political power inside it dwindling. In these cases, the argument for leaving the EU relied on representations of the UK as a minor actor ostracised by a more powerful and hostile European alliance:

Extract 7

If we vote to remain in the EU it will mean staying in a European Union where the UK can be automatically outvoted, where we can't veto unwanted regulations and where unelected judges can overturn more and more UK laws. That's why the safer option is to Vote Leave and take back control.

Notably, one of the most frequent argumentative schemes supporting the leave choice as an ideological resistance to a dominant 'ever closer Union' was supported by negative representations of the supremacy of the European Court of Justice (ECJ) 'meddling' with British affairs and with the British legal system. The goal premise of 'freeing Britain from the ECJ rule' derived from this representation spanned interdiscursively to warrant arguments of economic independence and of control over immigration. For example, the proposition that by leaving the EU Britain would avoid obeying the economic and financial rules imposed by the ECJ was predicated on discourses of the 'burden of red tape' and limitations to 'free trade' (cf. Extract 7 above). Similarly, negative representations of the ECJ ruling over the British government in relation to the attribution or removal of citizenship rights were frequently invoked in the leave campaign and acted as circumstantial premises along the macro argumentative scheme of 'loss of sovereignty' to legitimise the leave vote as in the following example:

Extract 8

If we vote to stay, EU judges will decide who gets British citizenship. The ECJ [...] has used EU citizenship to take more and more powers from the UK, including over whether criminals and illegal immigrants can stay, requiring social security to be paid to EU migrants, undermining the UK's border controls and expanding prisoner voting rights.

In most cases however, the argument about typical functions of the state (citizenship rights and border control) allegedly being taking over by the EU was a particularised discourse which conflated the remit of ECJ and European Convention on Human Rights (ECHR)[6] but which nevertheless appealed to popular imagination in discourses of 'border vulnerability'. This and other related arguments on the 'issue' of immigration are discussed in more detail in the next section.

4.2.5. Immigration-related arguments

Since VL was nominated as the official candidate for the leave side, its campaign increasingly focused on themes of immigration. Whilst still pushing an agenda for free trade and sovereignty, the imperative to 'take control' became discursively mobilised in favour of arguments that initially problematised immigration – albeit through a rather neutral stance – through the *topos of numbers* as in the extracts below:

Extract 9

More than a quarter of a million people came to the UK from the EU in the 12 months to September 2015 – the equivalent of a city the size of Plymouth or Newcastle in a year. If this rate continues for a decade, there will be more than two million extra people. Many immigrants contribute to our society. They also affect public services. Experts disagree on the overall effect.

Later in the campaign, however negative representations of immigration became increasingly prevalent and contributed to construct an overarching discursive scenario of 'moral panic' (Cohen, 2002) about immigrants. Against this scenario the leave choice was legitimised through *fallacies of risk avoidance* and *public safety*. Figure 5 exemplifies a typical argument circulated on the VL website (and widely echoed in the press) between late April and the referendum date, namely that the EU was secretly planning to give millions of Turks visa-free access to Europe.[7] The diagram clearly suggests the 'risky' option of staying in the EU by depicting Britain 'targeted' by over 80 millions of migrants from candidate EU countries, an argument that rests on the fallacious assumption of mass migration from those countries.

In some cases, VL's escalation of moral panic about migrants relied on conflating distinct representations of free movement of people within the EU and representations of illegal immigration, a strategy that had similarly being deployed by UKIP and which was epitomised by the infamous 'Breaking point' poster released a week before the referendum.[8] Figure 6 exemplifies a semiotic realisation of how this conflation of discourses occurred within the argumentative scheme 'if Britain remains in the EU, this will happen/continue'. The written text on the left recontextualises the argument in Extract 8 above on the numbers of EU migrants. In this case, however, the argument is reinforced via a visual association which clearly misrepresents freedom of movement exercised by EU citizens as what one would perceive as people illegally trespassing a border, an image which capitalises on irrational fear of immigration and which recontextualises wider discourses of Europe's reaction to the refugee crisis.

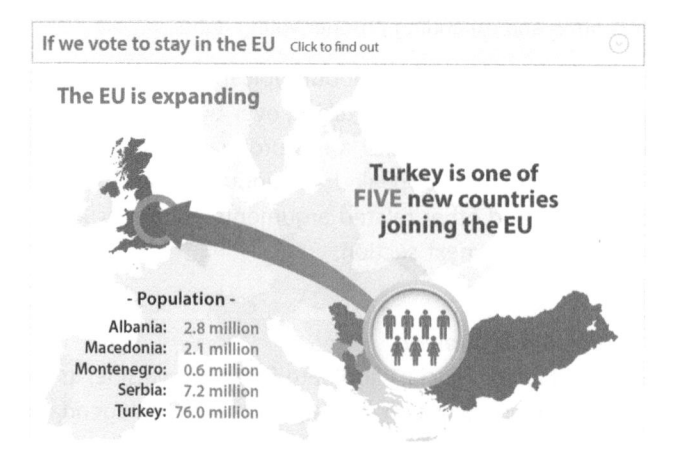

Figure 5. Misrepresentation of mass migration from EU candidate countries. Source: Why vote leave? The Facts. Retrieved 5 May 2016, from http://www.voteleavetakecontrol.org/our_case.html.

Immigration will continue to be out of control

Nearly 2 million people came to the UK from the EU over the last ten years. Imagine what it will be like in future decades when new, poorer countries join.

Figure 6. Misrepresentation of EU immigrants as illegal immigrants. Source: Why vote leave? The Facts. Retrieved 25 May 2016, from http://www.voteleavetakecontrol.org/our_case.html.

The moral panic about immigrants was also constructed through discursive scenarios focusing on the threat of terrorist attacks and border vulnerability with the thrust of the discourse provided by *topoi of security and public safety* which legitimised the leave choice as the ability to stop criminals entering Britain. In some cases, these arguments were realised through negative representations of the ECJ disempowering Britain (see Extracts 7 and 8 above) and on the goal premise of regaining control over immigration relying on a distorted logic that conflates immigrants with criminals and terrorists as in the following extracts:

Extract 10

Our border controls are under constant attack from the European Court of Justice (ECJ). Last year, the ECJ said that our Government cannot require migrants from other EU states to have a permit issued by UK authorities, even though permits from other EU countries are systematically forged, some EU countries sell their passports, and we have no control over the way other EU countries issue their passports. This makes it easier for terrorists and criminals to get into Britain.

Extract 11

Being in the EU makes it easier for terrorists to come to Britain - EU law forbids countries in the Schengen area from carrying out systematic checks on anyone with an EU passport from entering. This makes it much easier for terrorists fighting abroad to return to Britain, who need not pass through a single border control between arriving on the shores of Greece and reaching the English Channel. With terrorist groups launching attacks on Europe, more and more EU states are finding that they have to defy the EU and reintroduce border controls to keep people safe.

In these two examples the argument for leaving is supported by the main warrant that 'being in the EU makes it easier for terrorists to come to Britain'. This circumstantial premise is, in turn, articulated through different ambiguous premises (in Extract 9 the supposed corruption of other EU countries) or more explicit fallacies (Extract 10), the most obvious one being that the UK is not in the Schengen area and it has always retained the power to control its borders over movement of people from Schengen countries. The need to control borders which is invoked here to legitimise the leave choice seems to apply to a general openness of Europe (stretching 'from the shores of Greece to the

English Channel') and a perceived threat that such lack of borders would pose to Britain. However the representation of domestic security supposedly guaranteed by a system of international borders appears further contradicted by the representation of 'terrorists who return to Britain' if one assumes that such terrorists were British citizens in the first place and further highlights the contradiction of Britain wanting to be in control of its borders whilst expecting other countries to patrol them.

5. Conclusion: a toxic (inter)national logic of Brexit

This paper has illuminated the discursive legitimisation of Brexit in the messages of the official Leave/Remain campaigns, two key actors in the institutional framing of the referendum debate. It has highlighted how the institutional framing of the campaign allowed for two opposed camps to emerge and for specific discourses and interests to polarise around the 'in' and 'out' choices. The analysis has provided evidence of how trade and immigration acted as the two key discursive elements which drove the (de)legitimisation of Brexit appealing to both rational and emotional argumentative schemes. The analysis has also shown that BSE mainly engaged with economic topics focusing on discursive strategies which, on the one hand, highlighted the positive impact of Britain's membership of the EU on trade and jobs while, on the other, emphasised the risk of leaving the EU by projecting a series of negative consequences for citizens and households. Similarly to BSE, early discourses of the Leave campaign engaged with economic arguments. However, in contrast to BSE, VL's strategies were primarily aimed at delegitimising the EU as 'dominating' and 'constraining' the UK in its trading potential and 'meddling' with its national sovereignty. Becoming independent from the EU's antagonistic power provided thus the main legitimacy thrust to VL's discourses, which were typically realised via the 'take (back) control' slogan. Notably, as the campaign progressed, immigration increasingly gained currency in VL's discourses by becoming a central topic of the campaign. In this respect, VL's discursive strategies contributed significantly to the construction of the 'moral panic' of mass migration and, against this scenario, the legitimation of Brexit occurred through fallacies of numbers and public safety and through misrepresentations of the EU's freedom of movement.

The analysis has provided a body of evidence for a critical reading of Brexit showing that the choice over the UK/Europe relationship encapsulated in the vague binaries 'leave' and 'remain' acted as a powerful catalyst for the (de)legitimation of certain ideologies, the imagination of certain world orders, the reproduction of certain narratives of Britain and Europe.

Firstly, albeit from opposite grounds, the two campaigns largely framed the Brexit debate within representations of Europe as a zero-sum trading exercise. Whilst BSE relied on representations of the Single Market to legitimise the status quo as desirable for the UK, VL's campaign reproduced a neoliberal intergovernmental agenda advocating for a looser global trading system in which the UK could be a freer and much better-off actor taking advantage of global opportunities without the existing regulations of the Single Market. This vision, encapsulated in the *topos of sovereignty loss*, legitimised the leave choice as a matter of national interests to be safeguarded and pursued as much as an act of independence from the EU.

Secondly, by taking a nation-centric stance (i.e. speaking to and for the nation), the messages of the two campaigns largely reproduced historical conceptualisations of British-ness vis-à-vis a European 'other'. Whereas BSE accommodated the European (economic) narrative into that of the 'imagined' British nation, VL voiced a resurgent form of English nationalism by recontextualising discourses of a distinct British political and cultural exceptionalism which is not compatible with the European project. These representations were particularly prevalent in arguments supported by the *topos of national influence* which indexes different nation-centric views. Whilst, by and large, BSE represented national influence viable within a EU-ropean space and achievable through intra-national cooperation, VL used the same topos to argue for national independence and for forms of intergovernmentalism alternative to EU membership appealing to the narrative of Britain's glorious past and its economic and political global role.

Thirdly, VL recontextualised UKIP's anti-immigration agenda ideologically rooted in a divisive and populist reading of immigration as a problem of 'us and them' that governments must solve (Richardson, 2008) and reproducing a politics of identity which largely projects a sense of solidarity strictly within national rather than transnational boundaries. In this sense, representations of Europe in its cultural, civic, and social democratic dimensions were notably absent (see Zappettini, 2019a). Similarly, both referendum campaigns silenced the question of Scotland and Ireland reproducing a dominant English-centered vision of the internal cohesion of Britain. This discursive hegemony largely reflects the specific vested interests represented by the two organisations examined bringing into the public arena selected representations of Britain and/in Europe which contributed to the normalisation of (symbolic) borders and the relegitimation of national identities in the public opinion.

Crucially, the specific discursive articulation of trade and immigration emerged in the Brexit referendum campaign engendered and legitimised a new toxic (inter)national logic: by leaving the EU, Britain 'takes back control' to pursue mercantile policies whose benefits 'outsiders' should be excluded from. At a time of another major European crisis driven by populist and nationalist discourses, the Brexit referendum campaigns conspicuously failed to represent Europe in its social and supranational dimensions and to make the case for Europe as a transnational project of solidarity and social justice.

Of course, as the analysis has focused on the discourses of these two semi-institutional organisations, it would benefit from complimentary further investigation of how such discourses were received and consumed by other actors in other sites.

Notes

1. Designated campaigns were entitled to public grants (up to £7m), free mailing and broadcasts http://www.bbc.co.uk/news/uk-politics-360386721.
2. For details of endorsers see: https://www.electoralcommission.org.uk/find-information-by-subject/elections-and-referendums/upcoming-elections-and-referendums/eu-referendum/designation-of-lead-campaigners-for-the-eu-referendum.
3. These were www.voteleavetakecontrol.org (VL) and www.strongerin.co.uk (BSE).
4. For a discussion of free trade and its association with neo liberal ideologies in the context of Brexit see Zappettini (2019).
5. The figure was highly contested since it does not take into account a substantial rebate granted to the UK https://blogs.spectator.co.uk/2017/01/dominic-cummings-brexit-referendum-won/.

The pledge to spend £ 350 m on the NHS was dismissed by Leavers soon after the referendum result (http://www.independent.co.uk/news/uk/home-news/brexit-nhs-350m-a-week-eu-change-britain-gisela-stuart-referendum-bus-a7236706.html).

6. The ECHR was established prior to and independently of the EU in 1953 with the UK being one of its key promoters of its introduction. It has been adopted by a number of countries (including Turkey and Russia) which are not necessarily EU members states.

7. See for example https://www.thesun.co.uk/news/1271200/more-than-100000-turks-a-year-will-flock-to-britain-after-it-joins-the-eu-pushing-net-migration-to-a-staggering-420000/.

8. https://www.theguardian.com/politics/2016/jun/16/nigel-farage-defends-ukip-breaking-point-poster-queue-of-migrants.

Disclosure statement

No potential conflict of interest was reported by the author.

ORCID

Franco Zappettini ⓘ http://orcid.org/0000-0001-7049-4454

References

Bailey, O. (2016). *Argument or organisation? The battle over membership of the European Union. Fabian Society*. Retrieved from http://www.fabians.org.uk/wp-content/uploads/2016/04/Argument-or-organisation_-The-battle-over-membership-of-the-European-Union.pdf

BBC News. (2016). *The battle to be the official EU referendum Leave campaign*. Retrieved from http://www.bbc.co.uk/news/uk-politics-34484687

Chadwick, A., & Howard, P. N. (2010). *The Routledge handbook of internet politics*. London: Routledge.

Cohen, S. (2002). *Folk devils and moral panics: The creation of the Mods and Rockers* (3rd ed.). London: Routledge.

Cooper, A. (2016). The Brexit vote is history. A closed or open Britain is the defining battle now. *The Guardian*. Retrieved from https://www.theguardian.com/commentisfree/2016/jul/04/post-refe rendum-politics-eu-vote

Daddow, O. (2015). Interpreting the outsider tradition in British European Policy Speeches from Thatcher to Cameron. *Journal of Common Market Studies, 53*(1), 71–88.

Electoral Commission. (2016). *Electoral Commission designates 'Vote Leave Ltd' and 'The In Campaign Ltd' as lead campaigners at EU Referendum*. Retrieved from https://www.electoralcommission.org.uk/i-am-a/journalist/electoral-commission-media-centre/news-releases-referendums/electoral-co mmission-designates-vote-leave-ltd-and-the-in-campaign-ltd-as-lead-campaigners-at-eu-referen dum

Fairclough, N. (2003). *Analysing discourse: Textual analysis for social research*. London: Routledge.

Fairclough, I., & Fairclough, N. (2012). *Political discourse analysis. A method for advanced students.* London: Routledge.

Hilder, P. (2017). The revolution will be digitised. How politics got tangled up in the web. *Prospect Magazine*, pp. 32–36.

The Independent. (2016). *Vote leave designated as official EU referendum out campaign.* Retrieved from http://www.independent.co.uk/news/uk/politics/vote-leave-designated-as-official-eu-refer endum-out-campaign-a6982491.html

Jessop, B. (2017). The organic crisis of the British state: Putting Brexit in its place. *Globalizations, 14*(1), 133–141.

Kellner, P. (2016). Europe divides the country into two tribes like no other issue. *Prospect Magazine*, April Issue.

Koopmans, R., & Olzak, S. (2004). Discursive opportunities and the evolution of right-wing violence in Germany. *American Journal of Sociology, 110*(1), 198–230.

Krzyżanowski, M. (2010). *The discursive construction of European identities: A multilevel approach to discourse and identity in the transforming European Union.* Frankfurt am Main: Peter Lang.

Krzyżanowski, M. (2016). Recontextualisation of neoliberalism and the increasingly conceptual nature of discourse: Challenges for critical discourse studies. *Discourse & Society, 27*(3), 308–321.

Reisigl, M. (2014). Argumentation analysis and the discourse-historical approach: A methodological framework. In C. Hart, & P. Cap (Eds.), *Contemporary critical discourse studies* (pp. 67–96). London: Bloomsbury.

Richardson, J. E. (2008). "Our England": discourses of "race" and class in party election leaflets. *Social Semiotics, 18*(3), 321–335.

Savage and Cunningham. (2016). *Why inequality matters: The lessons of Brexit.* Retrieved from http://items.ssrc.org/why-inequality-matters-the-lessons-of-brexit/

Skinner, G. (2016). *Immigration is now the top issue for voters in the EU referendum.* Ipso Mori Survey. Retrieved from https://www.ipsos.com/ipsos-mori/en-uk/immigration-now-top-issue-voters-eu-referendum?language_content_entity=en-uk

Toulmin, S. E. (1958). *The uses of argument.* Cambridge: Cambridge University Press.

Vreese, C. H. (2007). *The dynamics of referendum campaigns: An international perspective.* Basingstoke: Palgrave Macmillan.

Wellings, B. (2007). Rump Britain: Englishness and Britishness, 1992–2001. *National Identities, 9*(4), 395–412.

Wodak, R. (2009). The discourse-historical approach. In R. Wodak, & M. Meyer (Eds.), *Methods of critical discourse analysis* (2nd ed., pp. 63–94). London: Sage.

Zappettini, F. (2019). The official vision for 'global Britain': Brexit as rupture and continuity between free trade, liberal internationalism and 'values'. In V. Koller, S. Kopf, & M. Milgbauer (Eds.), *Discourses of Brexit* (pp. 140–154). Abingdon: Routledge.

Zappettini, F., & Krzyżanowski, M. (2019). The critical juncture of Brexit in media & political discourses: from national-populist imaginary to cross-national social and political crisis. *Critical Discourse Studies.* doi:10.1080/17405904.2019.1592767

Zappettini, F. (2019a). *European Identities in Discourse: A Transnational Citizens' Perspective.* Bloomsbury: London.

'Out is out and that's it the people have spoken': uses of vox pops in UK TV news coverage of the Brexit referendum

Andrew Tolson

ABSTRACT

This article analyses vox pops in British television news programmes during the 2016 EU referendum. It is informed by a data set of 383 vox pops across the three main terrestrial TV news programmes: the BBC and ITV's News at Ten and Channel 4 News. A quantitative overview confirms two points made by [Greg Myers (2004). *Matters of opinion: Talking about public issues*. Cambridge: Cambridge University Press, namely that in vox pops the majority of respondents are anonymous, and their exchanges with journalists are minimal. However the argument here is that it is not appropriate simply to criticise vox pops as inadequate forms of political expression; rather a qualitative discourse analysis focuses on their use as illustrations in journalistic narratives, informed by changing news agendas. In the EU referendum, this often involved visits to provincial locations where the majority of respondents were Leave voters; and it culminated in visits to the communities of Brexit voters which can be seen as paradoxical. On the one hand they illustrated the cultural distance of these voters from the metropolitan elite; but on the other they gave voice to a populist political rhetoric widely reproduced in the Brexit public sphere.

1. Some critical perspectives on vox pops

This article offers an analysis of the use of vox pops in UK TV news coverage of the Brexit referendum. It covers a five-week period from the end of May 2016 to early July, that is just over three weeks before the referendum followed by ten days of its immediate aftermath. Recordings were made of evening news bulletins on the UK's three main terrestrial TV channels (BBC 1, ITV and Channel 4) resulting in a data base of 96 news programmes. This material has been used previously as the basis for a critical overview of journalistic strategies of reporting on the Brexit referendum (Tolson, 2018), but here just one strategy is in focus for a more detailed analysis. My intention is to develop further a critical perspective on the use of vox pops specifically related to Brexit news. In total there were 383 vox pops contained in 52 (or 54%) of the recorded news programmes, confirming that these are now a routine feature of British TV coverage of political elections – unlike some other European countries (Ekstrom & Tolson, 2017).

However, although this data does allow for some quantitative analysis, that is not the main aim of this article. Rather it has principally been motivated by some criticisms of vox pops made in the aftermath of the Brexit vote, by both academic and journalistic commentators. For example, in a booklet containing critical responses to media coverage of the EU referendum, produced by the UK's Political Studies Association, Professor Ivor Gaber (a former editorial advisor to the BBC Trust) criticised an 'over-reliance on the vox pop [where] a quick soundbite from a member of the public … gives the appearance of being representative but is probably atypical' (Gaber, 2016). And in a later opinion piece for *The Observer* Catherine Bennett referred to a warning from Roger Mosey (former editor of the BBC's radio programme *Today*) that 'this fetish for the vox pop too often squeezes out the space for analysis' (30th April 2017). Bennett's polemical argument criticises vox pops both for their opportunistic and unregulated methodology (unlike properly conducted opinion polls) and for their casting of journalists as quasi 'anthropologists' undertaking 'journeys into the British interior' (Bennett, 2017, p. 43).

There are some interesting points here which might indeed be of relevance to the Brexit referendum. However to fully appreciate that relevance it will be necessary to confront a major, perhaps dominant, perspective in political communication studies. This is an argument which under-estimates, in my view, the potential political significance of vox pops. It starts from some very reasonable observations: that there is a hierarchy of voices in TV news and that in this hierarchy the voices of 'ordinary people' are subordinated (Kleemans, Schaap, & Hermans, 2015). This is evident in the frequently anonymous and truncated format of vox pops as opposed to the lengthier 'news interviews' with opinion leaders and politicians.

What becomes problematic is a further argument that imports a normative theory of the public sphere as a central feature of democratic societies and is associated in particular with Jurgen Habermas (1989). For example Brookes, Lewis, and Wahl-Jorgensen (2004) refer to Habermas' argument about 'refeudalisation' of the public sphere as a 'helpful metaphor' by which to understand the difference between representations of elites (party leaders) and voters in TV news coverage of elections (p. 73). This is supported by studies of election news in other European countries, such as Hopmann and Shehata (2011) who argue that despite there being good reasons to include citizens in such news – 'to liven up stories, augment their authenticity and make them more understandable' – they remain 'one of those groups of actors that lack an inherent news value' as compared to elite sources such as 'high-level politicians' (p. 665). Citizens are included in stories on particular issues (such as welfare) where they 'are portrayed as spectators or victims rather than active participants in an ongoing debate', and these stories tend to occur later in news bulletins.

This Danish research concurs with earlier studies of US and UK news by Justin Lewis and his colleagues (Lewis, Wahl-Jorgensen, & Inthorn, 2004, 2005) which concluded that the identity given to ordinary citizens by the vox pop is that of consumers who comment on political issues as they affect them, rather than advocating policies or expressing concern for 'the common good' (2005, p. 88). This relates to an argument about the way citizens are represented, in vox pops, in both the US and the UK, as 'apolitical' individuals, who do not deliberatively engage with the public sphere (Lewis et al., 2004). Here the vox pop as a statement of opinion shifts to 'the impression of a citizenry unable or unwilling to put forward a political view' (p. 160), and as it applies to the UK, it is not just that citizen's opinions are of less news value, they are also shown to be very superficial; indeed 'ordinary citizens are almost childlike: they have moods, experiences and emotions, but they are rarely seen making forays into a deliberative public sphere' (Lewis et al., 2004). Brookes et al. argue that vox pops actually 'produce and perpetuate disengagement' where 'both the general public and particular populations … are alienated from politics' (2004, p. 75).

From the perspective of this article there are two main problems with this series of arguments. The first is a slippage from a critique of journalistic practice to the assumption that this reflects, and even helps to create, general political attitudes. Here the more polemical criticisms are also the most questionable. For example Bennett opens her piece with the notion of a reporter standing in the market piece of a northern city randomly accosting passers-by, and clearly Gaber just assumes that their statements are unlikely to be representative. (We shall see shortly why neither of these points can be true). But more particularly, as far as the Brexit referendum was concerned, a second problem is the argument about news value. Certainly the vox pops that appeared in the Brexit referendum news were usually anonymous and fragmented, but they were also highly newsworthy. Entire and repeated news stories were constructed around them. Arguably this is because a referendum, even more than a general election, gives the popular voice more significance than any other kind of political event.

2. Vox pops as minimal encounters

To begin to understand vox pops in more detail, it will be helpful to build on previous work which has studied them from a discourse analytic perspective. Particularly relevant here are two book chapters: an influential discussion of vox pops by Greg Myers (2004), also cited by Thornborrow (2015), and the aforementioned more recent international study of the reporting of the 2014 European elections which makes use of data from Sweden, France and the UK (Ekstrom & Tolson, 2017). Indeed some of the work for that chapter has influenced part of the analysis in this article. Taken together, what is clear from this discourse analysis is that there are firstly, variations in the vox pop format which allow for the production of different types of statement, and secondly, that vox pops are not at all the random encounters for which they have sometimes been criticised. As Montgomery (2007) has argued they are selectively chosen 'interview fragments' used to illustrate news reports.

Variations in the format of vox pops are apparent in the present study. In general terms, it is appropriate to define this format by highlighting key points of difference from other types of broadcast interview (on which of course there is a substantial body of work from a CA perspective). Thus unlike, for example, 'news interviews' vox pops do not involve interrogative sequences in which the interviewer (IR) can challenge the interviewee (IE). These are not 'accountability' interviews in Montgomery's terminology. Indeed in vox pops the questions are often unheard, and the IE is not introduced or sometimes even identified. So 'we don't know who we are listening to', according to Myers (p. 204). Furthermore, if sequences are constructed, this can involve 'the same question(s) asked to a series of people' rather than 'a series of questions to one person' (Myers, 2004). All of this offers a useful starting point for further investigation, but there are additional observations to be made.

In my data, it is indeed the case that in the majority of vox pops (275) the respondent was not identified and that in just over 50% (194) the question was edited out so that we only hear a single statement. In such cases the vox pop can perhaps be characterised as a type of 'soundbite'. However, that leaves about half of this data set where there is some verbal interaction, though this tends to be minimal. There are 61 interactions consisting of 2 turns (IR question – IE answer), 67 examples of 3 turns (IE-IR-IE) where the IR turn is a reaction or prompt, and 29 examples of 4 turns (IR-IE-IR-IE) where the IR asks a follow-up question. Of the total number of vox pops only 32 (8%) consisted of 5 or more turns and the longest one involved 8 turns. In this context some of the vox pops analysed by Myers (pp. 214–215) look to be untypical. With exchanges involving 11 and 12 turns they look more like conventional interviews than vox pops.

But there are two consequences of these variations. The first is that at least in some cases vox pops can be presented as *encounters* between members of the public and reporters (what kinds of encounter during the Brexit referendum will be discussed later). Secondly, where reporters as IRs are producing follow up questions and prompts, respondents (as IEs) are invited to clarify or expand upon prior statements. This entails more than an emotional or experiential reaction (such as those characteristic of eyewitness accounts). It can involve statements of opinion and indeed brief arguments where those opinions are justified.

As Montgomery argues, the selection of such 'interview fragments' is determined by the journalistic agendas they are used to illustrate. In a continuous event like a referendum (and its aftermath) these agendas have the narrative structure of updates to ongoing stories. For example during the Brexit referendum initial concern for the registration and turnout of younger voters was followed by a 'Labour heartlands' agenda when it became clear that some traditionally Labour supporting areas were likely to vote to leave. Some of these stories reproduced a point made by Myers that people are often chosen for vox pops because they apparently represent 'membership categories'. In Myers' now familiar formulation: the question in a vox pop is not 'what do you say' but 'what does someone like you say' – and it is 'the interviewee's job to figure out what 'someone like you' means in this case' (Myers, 2004, p. 209). In other words respondents are typecast (often visibly) and what they have to say is used to represent categories that fit into dominant journalistic narratives.

As Myers also illustrates, very often these categories are related to locations. So when a BBC reporter wants to investigate the turnout of black voters in a US presidential election, he visits the streets of Harlem. In the 2014 European election reports about 'euro-scepticism'in the UK involved visits to what were defined as 'UKIP territories', such as marginalised coastal and seaside towns (Ekstrom & Tolson, 2017, pp. 220–223). During the EU referendum the story about Labour voters took reporters to towns in South Wales and the Midlands (as the next section will illustrate). Interest in the Brexit result brought reporters to those (typically provincial, culturally conservative) areas where they were likely to find Brexit voters. There was nothing at all random, or even apolitical about this, as voters were specifically selected to give voice to their allegiances.

3. 'Labour heartlands': the vox pop spectrum

To illustrate the point about discursive variation, this section examines two sequences of vox pops from the 'Labour heartlands' in the Midlands. The first example has ITV's chief political correspondent Robert Peston accompanying Gordon Brown on a visit to Leicester; and here a clip of Brown's speech was preceded by a series of vox pops in Leicester market. These are used to test voters' knowledge of Labour party policy, and Peston does this by asking 'quiz questions' – that is the type of question designed to test a respondent's knowledge, sometimes put to politicians in election interviews (Clayman & Romaniuk, 2011). Peston's first four respondents fail the test, but he doesn't follow their answers with corrections. His only follow-up turns are with respondents (VP5 and VP6) where the initial answer is correct, but again in these exchanges the interaction is minimal.

	ITV News 13th June
	[Shots of Leicester market]
RP:	No it's not the European single market it's the covered market in Leicester where I've come to assess whether one important reason why the Leave side seems to be pulling ahead in the referendum battle is that too few people know Labour's position.
	Do you know where Labour stands on the referendum? Are they in or out?
VP1:	I should think they'd be out.
VP2:	I'm not sure either.
VP3:	They're they're leaving most of them.
RP:	Do you know where Labour stands on the referendum?
VP4:	Unfortunately no 'cos I'm still reading the facts to be honest.
VP5:	To remain in the UK.
RP:	Yes and do you know what you want to how you're going to vote?
VP5:	I'm going to vote definitely leave the EU.
VP6:	I think it will be in.
RP:	What about you personally where do you stand?
VP6:	I stand with Labour.
RP (v/o):	Yes in fact Labour is for staying in [clip of Gordon Brown speech "the European Union is not the cause of the problem"] And so I met this former Prime Minister who's trying to re-launch Labour's pro-EU campaign.
	[cut to Peston interview with Brown aboard a train]

The approach taken by Peston here would seem to conform to a practice previously described as 'the discursive production of ignorance' (Ekstrom & Tolson, 2017, p. 213ff). (In the EU election of 2014 similar questions were put to voters on what they knew about UKIP party policies). This is clearly one end of the vox pop spectrum where, because there are no follow-ups, there is no opportunity for respondents to state opinions, let alone make an argument. Even with respondents whose initial answer (to the unheard question) was correct, their second turns are not followed up, for instance by seeking explanations for their voting intentions. Rather with their ignorance, or at best uncertainty, respondents have been chosen to serve simply as a pretext for the subsequent interview with Brown (and of course he is introduced whereas the vox pops are anonymous).

It is also not particularly significant that these vox pops are in Leicester. For instance nothing is made of the fact that this is a city with an ethnically diverse population and of the six vox pops five are with ethic minority respondents. However, this is not reflected in the type of 'membership categorisation' to which Myers has referred. Essentially these just happen to be people in a city where Brown (and thus Peston) are visiting. But in other packages the location was significant, where journalists used vox pops to investigate the possible working class vote to leave. There were several such packages: for example Gary Gibbon for Channel 4 news in West Bromwich (9th June) and Walsall

(13th June), and Carl Dinnen of ITV in the 'Labour heartland' of Worksop (10th June). Here is another example in a second visit to West Bromwich, made by John Pienaar, the BBC's deputy political editor.

	BBC News 10th June
	[Shots of Polish food store and people of diverse ethnicity in the street]
JP:	Here in Labour West Bromwich the thing that's troubling voters is easy to see: migration into Britain celebrated by Labour politicians, disliked by so many of their voters. Appeal or no appeal who's listening? Try asking in the high street or on a visit to the local barber.
	[Cut to shot of Pienaar having his head shaved]
JP:	Mac where are you in or out?
VP1:	Erm I'm tending towards out mainly due to the immigration really. A lot of immigrants are coming in too fast for us to cope with.
JP:	What about a lot of immigrants working in the NHS and that's helping to make the NHS work?
VP1:	Well yes they're already in position. I'm worried about the ones coming through. I don't know whether we'd be able to cope with the amount.
	[Another customer at the barber's]
JP:	Are you in or out? Tell me why.
VP2:	I'm in. I think people need to work in partnership with other people. I think people who are voting out are voting out because of immigration and issues like that and I think that in the longer term it's going to affect the country.
JP:	[Shot of betting shop] Picking the winner in this referendum's anyone's guess. It's a gamble and Labour's finding it hard just to keep up. Another MP's joined the leavers:
	[Cut to interview clip of John Mann MP]
JM:	Probably a large majority of Labour voters are knowledgeably knowingly voting to leave and they're voting to leave because the European Union is broken. It's not working for the working classes in this country.
	[Cut to shots of café with Pienaar drinking tea]
JP (v/o):	In Labour territory if people don't vote to remain in Britain could go out. Over a brew you hear the same thing time and again.
VP3:	I'm out
JP:	You're out
VP3:	Yes
JP:	Why any particular reason?
VP3:	Yeh immigration's the main factor for my decision. Erm we do a lot we do a lot for oth- all countries around the world bailing them out of their problems when we've got homeless people in this country.
JP:	Are you a Labour supporter?
VP4:	Yes I am.
JP:	The Labour Party wants you to vote in.
VP4:	I'm sorry but I just can't I just can't. I'm out.
VP5:	Yeh I'm voting out.
JP:	Tell me why.
VP5:	Immigration. Yeh immigration.
JP (to camera):	Come here come almost anywhere deep in Labour territory and you can see why Labour In campaigners are telling me they're not just worried, they're scared. Fears of mass migration have grown, a lot of people just want to kick the establishment and poster slogans about taking back control can sound good if you're feeling overlooked or taken for granted ...

By comparison with Peston, Pienaar's interactions with his respondents, though still minimal (and thus not interviews) are more substantial. Of these five vox pops two involve exchanges of four, and one of five turns. There is also some opportunity here for respondents to produce opinions, particularly in response to Pienaar's 'why' question, but also in the context of an argument, illustrated by his exchange with Mac, the barber. And though the immigration issue was clearly emotive, it is surely not the case that VP1 or VP3 are simply personal reactions – they are (however we might want to disagree) broader societal and political arguments. VP2 extends this into a metacommentary on the 'issues' and potential consequences of a leave vote. In short some academic criticisms of vox pops, at least in packages like this, seem to be missing the point. There is certainly, as we have seen with Peston, an approach which can appear exploitative, but there is also the potential on some occasions for statements of opinion to be made.

However, let us return to the journalistic context for vox pops like this. Arguably, what is of critical importance here is not the form these statements take but the way they are interpreted. In part (and the political communication literature is right about this) this is indeed because the statements made by ordinary citizens have less status that those made by politicians, like John Mann, suitably captioned, in Pienaar's piece. But also, crucially, this is to do with the obvious fact that the vox pops, however, they are constructed, are framed by journalistic commentaries, usually made to camera. And the journalist's warrant for making such comments is that he or she has visited the community featured in the piece. The report is a dispatch from a selected location, where the reporter can be shown engaging in exchanges with locals which are only of interest in so far as they illustrate the narrative that he or she constructs. In this case, this even extends to some participant observation, as Pienaar is shown, not just on the street but also visiting the barber's, and drinking tea in a local café.

4. 'Exemplification' as ethnography

There is another theoretical perspective on the use of vox pops in political news which, though ultimately flawed, goes some way towards clarifying what might be happening in reports like Pienaar's. This is an approach from social psychology known as 'exemplification theory' and it starts from assumptions which are the opposite of those made in political communication studies. Here, far from being inconsequential or trivial, it is argued that the opinions expressed in vox pops have credibility because ordinary people are more likely to be trusted than experts and particularly politicians. This is because with their 'vividness, realism and distinctiveness' the voices of 'common people' can be taken as illustrative and thus 'representative of public opinion' (Lefevre, De Swert, & Walgrave, 2012, p. 105, p. 115). Here 'exemplification' seems to carry connotations of 'exemplary' particularly where these and other authors then proceed to hypothesise and test their assumption that vox pops perceived in this way are likely to have strong audience effects.

But we do not need to sink into the mire of effects measurement to recognise that representativeness is indeed a key feature of the journalistic use of vox pops. We are back to Myers' question: 'what does someone like you think', where 'you' might be a traditional Labour voter in a place like West Bromwich. Nor do we need to assume that their arguments about immigration were influential with the TV audience to recognise that they are presented by Pienaar as typical. Here journalists are visiting particular communities in search of opinions which are not so much exemplary as examples to be used in their narratives driven by news agendas. And nowhere was that this more evident than in the news that followed the referendum vote, as journalists went in search of the Brexiteers.

In the eight days following the vote (24th June–1st July) out of 24 news programmes, 19 contained sequences of vox pops. These covered a variety of topics – some directly related to Brexit such as its consequences for Scotland and the future of the Northern Irish border; and there were also vox pops on the political fallout, with Conservative voters being asked about future leaders and young Labour supporters about their endorsement of Jeremy Corbyn. However in the overwhelming majority of these programmes (p. 15) the chief concern was the reasons why people voted for Brexit, and this usually involved journalists visiting areas where the majority voted to leave. Thus Channel 4 News had sequences of vox pops with Leave voters in Cleethorpes (25th June) and Hartlepool (27th June) both conducted by its North of England correspondent, Ciaran Jenkins. The BBC dispatched Mark Easton to East Anglia to explore the differences between Leave supporting Peterborough and Remain supporting Cambridge (24th June). It also sent Sian Lloyd to South Wales to investigate the paradox of a Leave vote in a region in receipt of significant EU funding (26th June). ITV news sent its Social Affairs editor Penny Marshall on a tour of Leave constituencies including Boston (Lincolnshire), Mansfield (Nottinghamshire) and Blaby (Leicestershire). Her tour also took in Birmingham where the vote was evenly divided and the paradox was that some people from immigrant backgrounds voted to leave (28th June). However with this one exception what was notable was that most of these visits were not to major cities but to provincial towns and villages. And here another interesting feature of the vox pop became apparent – illustrated in my next example, which features the BBC's James Landale on a visit to Essex.

	BBC News 27th June
	[Shot of cargo ship off shore]
JL (v/o):	In Canvey Island trade with Europe and elsewhere is hard to miss. Yet this is a corner of the south Essex coast where the EU flag no longer flies, where almost three quarters of people voted to leave.
VP1:	Out is out and that's it the people have spoken. People are always going to feel a bit nervous after er about all the changes but at the end of the day you know what's done is done. And if we were to go back on that and start questioning the result then democracy is dead.
VP2:	We're Great Britain we're England we've been doing this for hundreds of years. I can't see us coming out of Europe causing any problems.
	[Cut to shots of café]
JL (v/o):	Here with their East End traditions and pie shops there's little regret at the vote for Brexit and the fact that it won't happen overnight.
VP3:	I don't know I think it's going to take a long time for change to happen but if it changes to how it was twenty years ago well that's for the good.
VP4:	If it was me I'd come out tomorrow.
JL:	(.) That's not going to happen though is it?
VP4:	No it aint going to happen my son. It aint going to happen.
JL (v/o):	But amid the optimism, a note of anxiety. Paul Masters a local businessman voted leave but
VP5:	It could be five years before we see the good side you know not tomorrow it's not going to happen tomorrow. It's not going to happen today you know it's (.) at least five years before (.) if it is a good thing and I'm still not sure it is a good thing. I'm still a little bit (.)

JL:	So you're having second thoughts.
VP5:	Not so much second thoughts but I just think I should have given it more thought.
JL (v/o):	Down the road at the Island café there was some concern that the leave campaign was appearing to row back on its promises. Are you confident that we're going to come out, immigration will stop er all that money they promised to the NHS are you confident that's [going to get spent?]
VP6:	Yeh they should do if they don't they're going to make themselves look stupid aint they? You know so if they don't do what they say well eh what's the point of saying it?
JL (v/o):	… Expectations are running high [shot of beach café] For now though many in Canvey Island are just content that their voices are being heard. James Landale, BBC news, Essex.

There are three aspects of Landale's report from Canvey Island that are worthy of comment. The first is to note again that he does not simply accost passers-by in the street, but, like Pienaar, visits shops, cafes etc. in the community. There he encounters some classic Brexit rhetoric typified in the populism of VP1, the nationalism of VP2 and the nostalgia of VP3 (she appears to be serving in the café) which are left as single turns without additional questions or responses. Interestingly however where Landale does interact with the follow up to VP4 and the question to VP6 he is presented with statements in the rhetorical form that Basil Bernstein once described as 'sympathetic circularity' (Bernstein, 1971). The use of tags like 'you know', the colloquial tag question 'aint they?' as well as the informal address ('my son') create the impression of a consensual relationship between his respondents and the journalist rooted in a collective appeal to 'commonsense'.

Except there is a third point, which is brought into focus by the exchange with VP5. Here the local businessman is clearly an exception, not only because he is named and might be having second thoughts, but also because of the way those thoughts (however incoherent) are expressed. There is a contrast between his use of what Bernstein called an 'elaborated code', with its suggestion of individual thinking, and the categorical statements made by the anonymous majority. Furthermore, the British viewer of this sequence will recognise the linguistic subculture shared by this anonymous group of Brexiteers. With their distinctive forms of address and colloquial tag questions they are speaking Cockney; an impression reinforced by Landale's reference to East End traditions and shots of the pie shop.

In short the additional dimension here is a form of *ethnography* with the journalist cast in the role of an explorer. This approach was also used in some vox pops with UKIP supporters during in the EU election of 2014 (see also Ekstrom & Tolson, 2017). In these vox pops respondents may be given some space to state opinions and to interact, however briefly, with journalists. The journalists themselves may be engaging with, indeed participating in, aspects of community life. But these relationships are contained within the narrative structure of the fleeting visit to another world, as determined by the dominant news agenda and the exigencies (timetable etc.,) of the construction of news programmes. In this format the journalist's address to the viewer (Landale uses voice over for this) defines the community not just as exemplifying an opinion, but also a (sub) cultural formation, where the former relates to the latter. This then becomes the focus for an ethnographic question: who were these people who, in their provincial communities, voted for Brexit?

5. Conclusion: peripheral cultures and populist politics

Only some of the vox pop sequences that followed the Brexit vote contained this ethnographic dimension and not all were as explicit as Landale's report from Canvey Island. It was more a case of variations on a theme, starting with verbal reminders about 'former mining communities' in the South Wales valleys (BBC News 26th June) and the 'mining heritage' of County Durham (BBC News 24th June). The filming that accompanied such locations ranged from long shots of industrial landscapes (Ebbw Vale) to a townscape of Durham with its iconic castle. Here the visual track that accompanied the voice over sometimes carried connotations of tourism – very evident in the contrast between Peterborough and Cambridge (BBC News 24th June) where shots of the former's historic cathedral were juxtaposed with predictable shots of university colleges and punting on the river Cam. Something more akin to the more engaged ethnographic experience of Canvey Island was on offer in Penny Marshall's report from Blaby (ITV News 29th June) where this part of 'rural Leicestershire' included a vox pop with a Leave voting horse breeder and shots of Morris dancers outside a country pub. But it was a report from Burnley on Channel 4 News (1st July) that truly epitomised and indeed confirmed the basic structure of the ethnographic vox pop.

Introduced by presenter Cathy Newman as a 'snapshot' this featured a photo-journalist, Peter Dench, visiting this industrial town in Lancashire. Shots of the location concentrated on streets of terraced houses and backstreets, to the mournful soundtrack of a bass band. His tour took in a practice session by the brass band as well as a Ladies' darts evening at a social centre and men of various ethnic backgrounds working out in a gym. A café owner with an Iranian background also explained his vote to leave. Interestingly however Dench's search for Brexit voters involved him conducting some vox pops on the doorsteps of terraced houses and thus occupying a space between public and private (the street and the front room). In each of these contexts, as a photo-journalist, he proceeded to take portraits presumably as a record of who these voters were and what they looked like. In this instant the journalistic report became a quasi-documentary in which these working-class Brexiteers were visually objectified.

No doubt that was an extreme case, but it also clearly illustrates a more general point. In many of the vox pops relating to the EU referendum, the structure involved an encounter, even a collision, between representatives of two cultural formations. On the one side were the inhabitants of provincial communities with their dislike of immigration and alienation from metropolitan politics. On the other there were the journalists sent to investigate these communities and report back to their newsrooms. Furthermore, immediately following the Brexit vote, as is common in moments of high political drama, the presentation of news shifted from the studio to iconic metropolitan locations, such as outside 10 Downing Street (BBC News 24th June) or the Palace of Westminster (ITV News 24th June). Here the programme structure visibly reproduced the cultural divide that prompted many people to vote Leave in the first place. It represented Brexit voters as localised and provincial, far removed from the centre of political power occupied by the metropolitan elite.

However there is also a paradox here which again is illustrated by Landale's report. Despite their distance from the cultural centre, most of his respondents in Canvey Island seem to feel empowered by the Brexit result. On the one hand then, they are objectified; but on the other, with their use of the collective 'we' and markers of sympathetic circularity, they are expressing an optimistic subjectivity, based on a belief as Landale puts it that 'their voices are being heard'. Of course a cynic might put some of this down to wishful thinking: for instance the assumption made by VP6 that Brexit supporting politicians are not going to break their promises. But also consider this: with his categorical argument about the will of 'the people' VP1 in particular is using exactly the same form of populist rhetoric that came to prominence in the post-Brexit public sphere. 'Out is out and that's it' has exactly the same tautological structure as 'Brexit means Brexit' where the language of 'the people' was being discursively reproduced by the British Prime Minister.

In short there is some evidence here of a convergence between aspects of the public sphere and populist discourse, facilitated by this journalistic use of vox pops. Now it might be possible to argue that this development is a form of 'refeudalisation' which displaces an ideally deliberative public sphere (a perspective expressed, in a way, by VP5). But for the majority of the residents of Canvey Island selected for Landale's piece there is no sugges- tion of voter disengagement. On the contrary, it can be argued that in at least some respects the post-Brexit public sphere is rhetorically aligned with this peripheral cultural formation (which puts the political elite in an interestingly unstable position – beyond the focus of this article). More specifically it might also require some revaluation of the use of vox pops in contemporary TV journalism. They may indeed, in Bennett's argument, amount to a form of 'anthropology' which 'squeezes out the space for analysis'. But they also illustrate political narratives that, at least in the Brexit referendum, had some poli- ticians mimicking voters in their use of populist forms of rhetoric.

Disclosure statement

No potential conflict of interest was reported by the author.

References

Bennett, C. (2017, April 30). Want to know what people really think? Don't do a vox pop. *The Observer*.
Bernstein, B. (1971). *Class, codes and control*. London: Routledge and Kegan Paul.
Brookes R., Lewis J., & Wahl-Jorgensen K. (2004). The media representation of public opinion: British television news coverage of the 2001 general election. *Media, Culture and Society*, 26(1), 63–80.
Clayman, S., & Romaniuk, T. (2011). Questioning candidates. In M. Ekstrom & M. Patrona (Eds.), *Talking politics in broadcast media* (pp. 15–32). Amsterdam: John Benjamins.
Ekstrom, M., & Tolson, A. (2017). Citizens taking politics in the news: Opinions, attitudes and (dis)en- gagement. In M. Ekstrom & J. Firmstone (Eds.), *The mediated politics of Europe: A comparative study of discourse* (pp. 201–227). London: Palgrave Macmillan.

Gaber, I. (2016). Bending over backwards: The BBC and the Brexit campaign. In D. Jackson, E. Thorsen, & D. Wring (Eds.), *EU referendum analysis 2016: Media voters and the campaign* (pp. 54). Poole: The Centre for the Study of Journalism, Culture and Community, Bournemouth University.

Habermas, J. (1989). *The structural transformation of the public sphere*. Cambridge, MA: MIT Press.

Hopmann, D. N., & Shehata, A. (2011). The contingencies of ordinary citizen appearances in political television news. *Journalism Practice, 5*(6), 657–671.

Kleemans, M., Schaap, G., & Hermans, L. (2015). Citizen sources in the news: Above and beyond the vox pop? *Journalism*, 1–18.

Lefevre, J., De Swert, K., & Walgrave, S. (2012). Effects of popular exemplars in television news. *Communication Research, 39*(1), 103–119.

Lewis, J., Inthorn, S., & Wahl-Jorgensen, K. (2005). *Citizens or consumers? What the media tell us about political participation*. Maidenhead: Open University Press.

Lewis, J., Wahl-Jorgensen, K., & Inthorn, S. (2004). Images of citizenship on television news: Constructing a passive public. *Journalism Studies, 5*(2), 153–164.

Montgomery, M. (2007). *The discourse of broadcast news: A linguistic approach*. London: Routledge.

Myers, G. (2004). *Matters of opinion: Talking about public issues*. Cambridge: Cambridge University Press.

Thornborrow, J. (2015). *The discourse of public participation media: From talk show to Twitter*. London: Routledge.

Tolson, A. (2018). Polarized politics and personalization: British TV news coverage of the EU referendum 2016. In F. Leon-Solis, A. Ridge Newman, & H. O'Donnell (Eds.), *Reporting the road to Brexit: International media and the EU referendum 2016* (pp. 111–126). London: Palgrave Macmillan.

Populism at work: the language of the Brexiteers and the European Union

Carlo Ruzza ⓘ and Milica Pejovic

ABSTRACT

This article investigates the recurring concepts emerging in a transnational social-media arena focusing on Brexit in the period immediately after the June 2016 referendum. It mainly focuses on a language/discourse analysis of Facebook posts by commentators interacting with the European Commission and the European Parliament. The article provides an ideological analysis of the main positions emerging in the transnational sphere of interactions between these two EU institutions and the wider public concerned with Brexit and active in a transnational discussion on a range of topics related to this process. It identifies the main issues that fueled British Euroscepticism, justifications for different attitudes towards Brexit and interrelations between opposite camps in the Brexit debate. It is argued that the contents of the debate emerging in the transnational arena identified vary considerably from the contents that were recurrent in the media and parliamentary debate. While the overwhelming framing in media and political discourse was focused on the migration issue, the debate emerging in the transnational arena appeared clearly focused on the legitimacy of supranational governance. It posits that this difference can be attributed to the make-up of the mini-public defined by the social networks interacting in debates on EU institutions.

Introduction

The year 2016 marked a turning point in European and International politics. A set of radical right populist parties made or consolidated electoral advances in several European countries. The election of Donald Trump in the US had important consequences, which included a loss of legitimacy and power of international institutions, such as the United Nations. A period seemed to be coming to an end, characterized by the decline of a cosmopolitan ethos in which nationalist forces appeared to be on the wane. Set in this context, the June 23rd referendum on Brexit appeared as a powerful broadside against the values of economic neoliberalism as embodied in the EU vision of a borderless Europe. The referendum results indicated a slight majority against continuing membership to the EU and come as a shock to the entire world as continuing membership of the UK within the EU was generally taken for granted. Although set in a broader context of advancing populist forces, the decision to leave the bloc still seemed inexplicable to most observers.

For decades, the UK had hosted probably the strongest and most widespread Eurosceptic movement. Nonetheless, the referendum outcome appeared surprising. It was after all the decision of a medium-sized country to leave the nearest, and for its economy most important, trading bloc, with which it had exchanged goods, people and services for many decades. Analyses of the vote revealed that the social groups that had propelled that decision were, on the one hand, older well-off voters and on the other hand, the groups that have come to be dubbed 'the losers of globalization'. That is, the 'leavers' were generally relatively poor and undereducated voters who were most likely to compete unfavorably with migrants and to work in economic sectors inundated by cheaper imported goods. In addition, this constituency felt that the currently dominant ethos of globalism, and the related substantial flow of migrants, which complements neoliberal policies, undermined their mainly localist cultural identity (Inglehart & Norris, 2016).

The referendum result was then a particularly strong manifestation of a larger and gradually emerging trend towards protectionism, a reassertion of nationalist values and a nostalgic evocation of more cohesive nation-states. This outlook is of course rejected by cosmopolitan constituencies who embrace and possibly benefit from processes of European integration. Such opposite views have led to a sustained and highly conflictual debate, which has taken place in several discursive public arenas, ranging from typical political arenas to workplaces, intermediary associations and the media. It has of course been a debate that has marked the political and cultural life of the UK for decades, and whose results have been powerfully shaped by a distinctive type of right-wing tabloid press, which has characteristically endorsed the identification of Europe and migration (Balch & Balabanova, 2017). However, we cannot assume that the cultural frames that have justified Brexit in various sectors of the population are the same as the frames sponsored by the press that encouraged it. Other arenas have distinctive structural features and contents that need to be examined.

One such arena occurs in a transnational space and is constituted by debates often taking place in social media, or in web spaces administered by international institutions. Over recent years, processes of supranational cultural and political integration have in fact led to the formation of a transnational public sphere, where these protectionist and localist values and the related Euroscepticism are also as likely to emerge as a cosmopolitan outlook. A transnational sphere is then emerging, and in the EU context is likely to constitute an arena of discussion and controversy over the scope and value of European integration (De Wilde, Michailidou, & Trenz, 2013; Michailidou & Trenz, 2015). Nonetheless, the analysis of this transnational discursive space is still in its infancy. An analysis of discourse in transnational spaces is essential, as it can shed light on emerging power relations, the particularities of these arenas and processes of constitution of transnational social fields (Beciu, Mădroane, Cârlan, & Ciocea, 2017).

The relationship between the EU and traditional news media has often been defined either as 'hostile' or 'indifferent' (Michailidou, 2017), while EU issues have been framed and interpreted through a national lens, without a pan-European, transnational perspective (Michailidou & Trenz, 2013). However, social media play an important constitutive role within transnational discursive spaces and boost the creation of a European public sphere. On the one hand, they are easily accessible by a large section of the population. Thus, in principle, Facebook-mediated communication could contribute to the development of the often-bemoaned lack of a demos so often lamented by democratic theorists studying the EU. It could enrich the number of arenas that democratic theorists argue are necessary to support the construction of a viable European demos and enrich other forms of internet-mediated political participation (Aichholzer & Strauß, 2016; Cheneval & Nicolaidis, 2017). Even more usefully, transnational participation in social-media arenas could help overcoming ethno-cultural, linguistic and geographical boundaries that are one of the main cause of the weakness of a shared European identity. Furthermore, participation in transnational arenas is important to anchor national identities to a positive vision of the European project (Fernández, Eigmüller, & Börner, 2016). In addition, ideally, a transnational space that allows a direct contact between EU institutions and the general public could alleviate the bias implicit in much elite discourse and media discourse, particularly in countries where the media have a generally negative attitude towards the European project. It could provide a recognizable and coherent alternative view of the EU, which would be resonant with the European public (see Krzyzanowski, 2018, p. 20).

On the other hand, however, this enabling role is rarely actualized. This is partly because the EU presence in social media tends to characterize itself as mainly aiming at an informational role rather than truly communicative one and because of a rather ineffective but recurrent discursive template of the EU, which tends to describe itself in policy and humanitarian action (see Krzyżanowski, 2015, 2018). It is also because only a small set of participants in key political debates chooses to interact in this transnational sphere. This characterizes them as distinct, identifying them as different from the constituencies that interact in mainly national-level political debates. In particular, the participants that interact with European institutions are both strongly motivated to reach a wider transnational public and politically aware of the structure of transnational arenas. We have then specifically focused on Facebook and the interactions of the European Commission and the European Parliament on issues of Brexit. The Commission and the Parliament interact with the wider European public and with a set of social-fora participants that are aware of the existence of this discursive opportunity and wish to reach a larger European public. By focusing on this segment of Facebook users, we are able to tap into a socially important and under-research sector of the European population. While Twitter, as a tool for the Europeanisation of political engagement on social media, has been more extensively analyzed than Facebook (Krzyzanowski, 2018; Barisione & Ceron, 2017; Barberá, Vaccari, & Valeriani, 2017), Facebook has been emerging as a leading forum for discussions. This is due to the ever-increasing practice of commenting on the pages of various socially engaged actors such as politicians, public institutions or the media (Bossetta, Segestean, & Trenz, 2017; Tarţa, 2017). Neverthless, research on Brexit and its role in Facebook debates is still very limited and mainly focuses on debates within the UK (see for instance: Del Vicario, Zollo, Caldarelli, Scala, & Quattrociocchi, 2017).

British Euroscepticism and Brexit

Since the outset of the UK's membership in the European Communities (EC) in 1973 and later in the European Union (EU), there has been little enthusiasm and conviction about the process of European integration among many Britons and their political elites; as the headline on the Guardian's front page from 1 January 1973 reads: 'We're in – but without the fireworks'. The country has been frequently labelled as a reluctant or 'awkward' partner (George, 1990), and two referendums on the EU membership prove this firmly embedded British Euro-hesitancy. Although the British government opted for the accession to the EC without asking for popular consent, it held a referendum on the withdrawal from the Communities already in 1975, which resulted in a robust support for staying in. However, in the 2016 referendum,the 'Leave' option won by 52% to 48%, ushering in the UK's withdrawal from the Union, which is planned for March 2019 when two-year negotiations are scheduled to be finalized.

British Euroscepticism is a multifaceted social construct present at the level of public opinion, party system, and the media. As a result of a particularly high level of scepticism towards European integration among the British, Eurobarometer has conducted aspecial survey dedicated solely to public opinion in the UK. The survey report, published in 2011 and titled 'Attitudes towards the EU in the UK' (EB Flash, 318), revealed a remarkably low level of knowledge on the EU, as only 18% of respondents felt informed about EU affairs. Respondents felt that the media reported too negatively on the EU, particularly the written press, and almost half of them observed a negative bias in press releases. The Spring 2016 Eurobarometer, which gauged public opinion on the EU immediately before the British referendum, shows the UK citizens who had a totally negative image of the EU (36%) outnumbered those who had entirely positive associations on the EU (31%). Moreover, according to the same opinion poll, 59% of UK respondents thought that their voice had not counted in the EU.

Although Euroscepticism has not been an exclusive characteristic of the British press, it is widely accepted that most British tabloid newspapers are strongly characterizedin terms of both the quantity and the negativity of framing of the EU. Euroscepticism has been a pervasive trait of tabloids such as *The Sun* and *the Daily Mail*, as well as of certain broadsheet newspapers such as *The Times* and *The Daily Telegraph* (Daddow, 2012). These newspapers frequently spread what have come to be known as Euro-myths – the term coined to denote a series of distorted or false news, which appear particularly present in British tabloids. Indeed, some scholars view the Eurosceptic press as one of the main culprits for public distrust towards the Union (Carey & Burton, 2004).

The questions of sovereignty and national identity have been particularly prominent in the British public debate on the EU (Diez Medrano, 2003). As a country with a long democratic tradition and a Parliament which is sometimes described as the 'mother of Parliaments' the UK has been particularly concerned about the alleged democratic deficit of the Union. On the other hand, a number of scholars argue that the UK's historic legacy and geographical location have contributed to its exceptionally high and persistent level of distrust and scepticism towards the process of European integration. Moreover, the Second World War, which for the majority of European countries was a traumatic experience, was a moment of military glory for Britain, as the country was neither conquered nor occupied, and, thus, has shown little appreciation for the EU as a peace and reconciliation project (Grant, 2008). Furthermore, an important factor that contributed to British Euroscepticism and its isolationism with respect the rest of Europe have been the country strong ties with Commonwealth countries and the U.S.A, particularly due to the shared language, cultural commonalities, and security arrangements.

Furthermore, the UK's imperial past has extended the country's political and economic aspirations beyond the European continent and in the common imaginary offered in the

Commonwealth an alternative community of reference – a community that has been interpreted differentially by the left and the right in terms of obligations and opportunities (Baker, Gamble, Randall, & Seawright, 2008). Finally, there is a UK exceptionalism based on the presence of Euroscepticism in both main political parties, whereas other European Eurosceptic parties have been generally marginal and mainly belonging to the family of anti-system protest parties (see Forster, 2002; Daddow, 2013). For instance, in the pre-Maastricht era the Labour Party was dominantly Eurosceptic and campaigned for the withdrawal at the time of the 1975 referendum, as the EEC were perceived as a pro-business, neoliberal project deprived of social welfare elements. Since the beginning of 1990s and the Maastricht Treaty, the perception of a threatened sovereignty and national identity has fuelled Euroscepticims among the Conservatives, and, consequently, spurred the emergence of the radical right, notably the UKIP (Ford & Goodwin, 2014).

Methodology

The methodology utilized consists of a 'frame analysis', that is, a type of content analysis of political documents developed and extensively utilized by social movements scholars to identify and assess the relevance of specific ideational contents and relational aspects of political texts. As the name of the methodology indicates, it focuses on framing as mechanisms of thematic inclusion and exclusion. It is an approach that since the early eighties has most consistently attempted to systematise the discursive elements that social movements attempt to utilize in order to achieve successful mobilization (Ruzza, 2006). In this tradition, frames consist of a set of cultural items that are used to define a situation in terms that are favourable to social movements – that is, conducive to political engagement and activation of a protest repertoire (Snow & Benford, 1988). The concept of the frame refers then to a central organizing idea that defines for an audience what is important in a debate. Frames also generally specify the causes of a problematic situation and indicate solutions. Movement frames stress the importance of active individual engagement, also often positing the existence of an injustice that needs to be remedied.

As mentioned, the reason for using this approach is that we conceptualize the process of Brexit mobilization as akin to a social movement, which is based on a restricted number of themes and connections among these themes, which are recurrent in a social movement community. Brexit was spurred by a distinctive ideology, a geographical identification both in terms of an 'imagined community' and in terms of exclusionary processes. It implied a conceptualization of the 'people' in classic populist terms, and is in this sense akin to other radical right populist movements (Hobolt, 2016; Clarke & Newman, 2017; Curry, 2017; Freeden, 2017).

Like all social movements, the number of themes that are utilized as discursive strategies varies in different arenas. They vary in different contexts according to factors such as the prevalent political culture of a nation, or of a particular discursive medium, or the changing political opportunities of a specific geopolitical context. For instance, a comparison of the dominant frames used in the texts of a set of different national peace movements reveals the differential impact of institutions such as the Catholic Church, or of legalistic understanding of political issues in different European national contexts (Ruzza & Bozzini, 2006). Thus, a frame analysis identifies which are the specific recurring themes in a specific context and helps addressing the question of why the same movement articulates its claims differently in different arenas. Similarly, by applying this methodology to social-media texts addressed to EU institutions, one can identify the structural features of the discursive contest that takes place in a transnational discursive sphere.

Framing theorists concentrate on the operating mechanisms of these arenas and examine topics such as the formation of mobilizing ideas, the responses of opponents, and the processes of re-definition that mobilizing ideas undergo under the influence of movement allies and institutional environments. Likewise, we will focus in a similar manner on the interaction between European institutions and the public. Frame analyses take different approaches in terms of preferences for more quantitative or more interpretative methodologies of frame identification. In this work, we will not specifically quantify the number of frames we have identified. Processes of quantification are often marred by reliability problems and in this case, high numerical accuracy does not seem relevant (Vicari, 2010; Cornelissen & Werner, 2014; Monforte, 2014). However, we have identified and commented the prevalent frames, which emerge in the Facebook comments. In practice, we have first read a sample of texts and formulated hypotheses on the recurrent themes. We have then 'condensed' these themes in short sentences that act as exemplars with which another sample of texts are scored. Every time a concept emerges that could persuasively be substituted with the exemplar, an instance of the frame is noted. The scorers – in this case the two authors of the article – act independently and then compare readings to achieve a reliably consistent interpretation of the texts. The process is however not one of the mechanically counting instances, but it aims to retain substantive access to the texts through ongoing and comparative access to excerpts.

As regards the choice of materials for our analysis, two Facebook posts have been sampled which were published by the Commission, and nine Facebook posts published by the Parliament. These posts were tightly related to the referendum results and mainly contained statements released by EU officials regarding the Brexit vote. As regards the temporal context, the sampled posts and comments were published during the first week after the Brexit referendum, from the 24th till the 30th of June 2016. This time frame has been selected in order to capture the immediate public reactions to the referendum results and reveal the reasons behind the Brexit vote. Furthermore, we selected 1537 comments, which were published by Facebook users as reactions to these eleven posts and which represent a lively transnational debate focused on the issue of Brexit, its causes, and its implications for the future of the Union. Initially, the number of comments to these posts was higher, but using the technique of purposive sampling, we reduced the batch to only those reactions clearly related to Brexit. Our main units of analysis are comments that Facebook users publish as reactions to the posts of the administrators of the Commission's and the Parliament's Facebook pages or comments of other interlocutors in the debate. We argue that the debates we analysed are transnational due to their unique language of discussion and the topic, which oversteps the UK borders. Since English has become the world's lingua franca, the fact that the Facebook pages of the Parliament and the Commission are managed in English enhances the transnational character of the debates that unfold on these pages and broadens the range of potential participants. Consequently, over 90% of the popular reactions to the selected posts published by the two EU institutions are in English. In addition to them, we coded the comments in the languages we are acquainted with (Italian, French and Spanish). As regards the transnational character of the topic of the recorded debates, we argue that Brexit referendum was both a British and European issue. Therefore, it is necessary to analyse these transnational discursive battlegrounds where different readings of the role of the UK in the EU and the process of European integration in general are discussed by regular citizens coming from the UK, the rest of Europe and beyond.

The analysis of these spontaneous and unsolicited online contributions portrays citizens' reactions to the unprecedented event of a country exiting the Union and complements but also redefines the findings of the more frequently conducted studies based on news media contents, political elites' discourses or public opinion surveys. It seeks to identify the most prominent frames that these lay commentators utilized to explain or justify the reasons for Brexit, or for their own Leave vote in case they were British citizens.

Findings

Considering the interaction between EU institutions as a whole, the frame analysis revealed that the discussion tends to be monopolized by Eurosceptic British participants. This shows how at least parts of the Brexit constituency, which is generally described as insular, can in fact be able and willing to bring the debate to an international forum. Only relatively few posts were supportive of the Commission and Parliament positions (approximatively one fifth). We then focussed on comments that were supportive of Brexit and that appeared to come from a British audience. That is, they often identified themselves as British, or made explicit references to their UK roots.

The arguments used by these commentators can be subsumed under the following three frames listed in order of descending frequency: the EU's alleged democratic deficit, the EU as a 'super-state', and the putative self-serving character and corruption of EU institutions. Questioning of EU democratic credentials was the most commonly used frame to substantiate British Euroscepticism, which is a surprising finding as the two issues that dominated the pre-referendum campaign were immigration and the economic consequences of Brexit (Hobolt, 2016). Furthermore, the overarching frame that permeates the entire post-Brexit debate we sampled were articulations of the 'people versus elites' cleavage. By expressing this frame, EU citizens voice their opposition to 'elites', who are generally understood as EU elites, but frequently the term 'elites' embraces also other categories such as national leaders, financial elites, multinational corporations or businesses. This proves the populist character of the Brexit constituency. In the following paragraphs, a more detailed illustration of these findings is provided.

Democratic deficit as the major concern

In the sampled post-Brexit Facebook debate, the EU was depicted as an evidently undemocratic political entity, and its lack of representativeness, accountability, transparency and responsiveness to public needs were mentioned as the main reason for the withdrawal of Britain. The EU was repeatedly qualified as a 'dictatorship', an 'undemocratic monster', an 'autocracy', an 'empire', or a 'plutocracy'. The EU set-up was frequently compared to illiberal regimes such as communism, fascism, or Nazism, and, consequently, Brexit was framed as 'liberation' from 'EU shackles' and the restoration of power of British people to decide on their own destiny. The examined post-Brexit debate is permeated by 'revolutionist' sentiments as the exit from the Union is perceived as a result of people's rebellion and popular backlash against dominantly pro-EU political elites. The following comment provides an illustration of popular resentment against the EU:

> OUT IS OUT! You can keep your EU we have our country back from the evil undemocratic totalitarian fascist communist dictatorial HORRID EU … We are a sovereign country and we will never ever be bullied by the EU and we've proved that! (Facebook page of the Parliament, 25/06/2016)

These frames echo similar positions voiced by the pro-leave campaign in the media, which conceptualized Brexit as a restoration of British freedom – a frame widely used by political leaders of the Leave camp, who were expressing nationalist sentiments in the context of instrumental evocation and political interpretation of historical events. For instance, Nigel Farage the leader of the most radical pro-Brexit campaigning organization – declared immediately after the referendum results that 23 June 2016 should be renamed the UK's 'Independence Day'.

According to some commentators in our sample, another sign of the alleged undemocratic character of the EU was its institutional set-up and the necessity of a reallocation of powers among its main institutions. The Commission was framed as the most contested EU institution which is frequently accused of being undemocratic, unaccountable, and excessively bureaucratized, while the Parliament was characterized as too weak and deprived from the right of legislative initiative. Furthermore, the EU decision-making process was framed as a cause of popular distrust towards the process of European integration, as it was portrayed as non-transparent, closed-door, and opaque.

Public dissatisfaction with EU democratic credentials has been also fuelled by an already well-established practice of repeating referendums on EU issues after 'no' votes. Commentators frequently referred to a series of repeated EU-related referendums as evidence that the EU 'ignored' negative results and overrode the democratic choice made by the Irish, the Dutch and the French by holding new referendums in Ireland or by 'disguising' the failed Constitutional Treaty into the Lisbon Treaty and adopting it without further consultations with the public. Similarly, commentators utilize a neologism 'neverendum', a term present in public parlance and used to denote the tendency of repeating EU-related referendums until obtaining a popular approval. The following comment is an example of the popular criticism towards the EU history of referendums:

> You mean like the constitution that got rejected by both French and Dutch voters, then slightly altered and without a single vote was adopted as the Lisbon treaty. That's the sort of history that misses one vital ingredient - a respect for democracy. An appalling history. (Facebook page of the Parliament, 29/06/2016)

In addition to the specific remarks regarding the set-up of EU institutions and Treaty changes, the post-Brexit online interaction contain numerous references that the EU 'lacks the people' and that ordinary citizens, who seek to reach EU institutions using social media, feel voiceless and excluded from EU decision-making. Although utilitarian and identity-based explanations of public Euroscepticism are preponderant in comparison to other hypotheses, the EU's democratic deficit has also been identified by some scholars as a major cause of negative sentiments towards European integration. For instance, McEvoy (2016) finds that political efficacy is the key determinant of popular attitudes towards the EU and that citizens who feel represented and heard at the EU level tend to continue supporting the EU even if their personal or their country's economic conditions worsened. Her analysis appears to confirm previous findings, which relate perceptions of political representation to attitudes towards European integration (Rohrschneider, 2002).

Another argument invoked in order to endorse Brexit, and connected with the issue of EU democratic deficit, was the alleged German political and economic domination of Europe, which was typically personified by negative references to German Chancellor Angela Merkel and her significant influence over decisions taken in Brussels. Many commentators who characterize the EU as undemocratic refer to the dominant role of Germany in intergovernmental decision-making processes and, thus, confirm in their views a growing perception that Germany is an emerging 'hegemon' in Europe, which is stifling other nations.

Incidentally, considering briefly the pro-European position, one notes that the democratic credibility of the referendum and its results were brought into question by a substantial part of online commentators. Whereas the Leave supporters have qualified the people's will expressed through the ballot box as an ultimate embodiment of democracy, the fewer comments of the opposing camp persistently contest the results and the pre-referendum campaign in terms of its lack of democratic qualities.

As Scotland and Northern Ireland voted overwhelmingly to remain in the EU, it was argued that the results of the referendum impinged on their democratically expressed will, hence, these two British constituencies were not bound by the outcome of the referendum. Moreover, it was suggested that the referendum was advisory and hence not legally binding, and that its results might be reconsidered due to the allegedly unfair campaign, allegedly plagued by misinformation and deception. Others warned that the tight referendum result reflected a highly polarized society and that it was dangerous to take a decision carrying such long-term consequences on the basis of such small difference in the number of votes between the two options. Additionally, the democratic legitimacy of the referendum was challenged with reference to the 28% of British citizens who did not vote, belittling in this way the victory of the Leave camp.

The sequent comment offers an informative insight into the group of arguments that contest the referendum process and campaign:

> Many millions of British citizens, as well as other UK residents, are feeling despair at recent events. A referendum which became, in the media, a single-issue "debate" centred only around "immigration" and economics, with shamefully inaccurate claims and counter-claims on both sides of the campaign, an almost total lack of objective information, and a base appeal to the fears of sections of society who feel frustrated by the decisions which their OWN GOVERNMENT have made, is a travesty of the democratic process. If only our own parliamentarians were to stand up for the rights of their people, this referendum could be cast out. This result shows that the country is governed by the press, not the politicians. (Facebook page of the Parliament, 29/06/2016)

The EU towards a 'super-state'

The vote for Britain exiting the EU was also framed as a consequence of the way the process of European integration extended far beyond the original idea of creating a common market among European states and safeguarding peace. The notion of being a part of a project that was supposedly heading towards a political union or a 'super-state' was often seen as particularly repulsive. The sequent comment reflects the ingrained British aversion towards a European political union:

> We do not need this forced political integration. We need a trade and cooperation union, not deeper political union. The entire EU project has ignored the will of the people for too long and now people are going against it. The EU cannot continue on the same path. (Facebook page of the Parliament, 26/06/2016)

One commentator explains his fear of a tighter political integration, cultural assimilation, and concerns about democracy in the following way:

> Culture and nationality should not be swept aside as though they don't matter. The world is a wonderful place. There are some fabulous people in it but it is impossible for one body to look after the needs and interests of 28 different countries, each with their own requirements. Why would you want to stifle 28 countries under one umbrella.. It started as a trade deal between 8 or 9 countries but it got very greedy and very distant and started meddling in all aspects of life until it became a federal state. Democracy all the way for me … and that's why I voted to leave. (Facebook page of the Commission, 25/06/2016)

Commentators often argue that the enfeebling of self-government caused by the necessity of pooling sovereignty among EU nations aggravated public unease about the future of the nation-state and its institutions, and undermined the trust of citizens that their country is still able to meet their basic needs. Economic and security instability – caused by recent financial and sovereign debt crises, massive migration inflows, and a disquieting number of terrorist attacks across Europe – have made the idea of 'taking back control' appealing not only to the British, but also to a substantial part of European publics, who increasingly view open borders as a dangerous threat.

EU institutions as 'main culprits'

As the UK has been a traditionally neoliberal country with a deep-seated aversion to bureaucracies, it is not surprising that the third most diffused frame used to explain the Brexit vote were the deficiencies of the set-up and functioning of EU institutions, which are described as overly bureaucratic, corrupted, opaque, self-serving, or colloquially as 'gravy trains'. Moreover, EU policies, as the main output of EU institutions, were repeatedly described as excessively regulatory and intrusive: commentators frequently referred to EU regulations regarding the regulation of items such as showerheads, vacuum cleaners, oil cans or bananas and their alleged preposterousness. In addition to the recurrent misrepresentations of certain EU regulations by the media and the creation of some very persistent myths, such as the EU rule regarding the curvature of bananas, it should be noted that an additional layer of regulations created in Brussels is considered at odds with deregulation – one of key neoliberal tenets and the integral part of the British socio-economic system since the era of Margaret Thatcher, and an integral part of the political culture of contributors to the Facebook debate. Moreover, EU institutions' tendency to rely on the expertise of their civil servants and agents was belittled by some Brexiters. This appears to reflect the opinion of politicians prominent in the Brexit debate, such as Michael Gove, who claimed that 'the people' were 'tired of experts'.

In the post-Brexit Facebook debate, EU institutions are portrayed as focused on their self-interest and/or the promotion of private interests and, thus, negligent in terms of their duty to focus on the public good. For instance, one commentator describes the EU as 'a rich club dictating policies to benefit corporation and banks and -most of all- THEM-SELVES' (bloc capitals in the original). As mentioned, EU institutions are also accused of being 'gravy trains' and of wasting time and tax payers' money on putatively pointless decisions or perpetual moving of the European Parliament:

> They don't seem to have any sense of reality - that might be why they spend time on discussing cinnamon in cakes - and spending billions a year moving offices once a month! A real disgrace spending money that way. (Facebook page of the Commission, 29/06/2016)

The Commission emerged as the most frequent target of popular dissatisfaction with the EU, mainly due to the lack of possibility of voting out the Commissioners. The following excerpt illustrates criticism towards the Commission's unaccountability and unresponsiveness:

> Brussels is unaccountable and undemocratic, we cannot vote or rid ourselves of EU Commissioners and they refuse to listen to the concerns of ordinary people, had they listened things could have been very different. There was, and still is, an opportunity for compromise, friendly consensus and co-operation but the President of the EU Commission's attitude so far sadly does not bode well for this. I am sad that so many people are making so many assumptions of why people voted to leave and not to remain. Yes there are nationalists, yes there are racists we know about them because they shout loudly but the vast majority of British people are quiet, decent, fair and generous and so I find your attitude quite insulting. Oh and for the record, I actually love European and am pretty damn fond of Europeans too! (Facebook page of the Commission, 29/06/2016)

Yet, the final sentences of the comment reflect the observation that Brexiters are frequently dismissed as nationalists or racist without entering into the merit of their dissatisfaction with the EU. The present analysis, however, seeks to overcome these generalizations and simplifications of public attitudes towards European integration and investigate the types of public concerns that motivated the Brexit vote.

People versus elites

The overarching frame of the Facebook debate analysed is the cleavage between the people and elites, since the Brexit vote was framed as a popular backlash against the distant and unresponsive political class, whether against those located in Brussels or against pro-EU politicians in London. Many online contributions to the post-Brexit debate stress the alienation of ruling political classes and the gap between citizens and politicians convening in 'glass towers' who supposedly dismiss popular concerns:

> I have just seen 49 percent of Austrian people also would leave EU without real reform if there is a possibility a referendum there too. EU definitely has to start to listen to its citizens before it is going to lose them. Nobody feel safe in their own country … . Politicians seemed to be isolated themselves from the public … this why they are surprised of the result of referendums. (Facebook page of the Commission, 30/06/2016)

In addition, throughout the post-Brexit Facebook debate, commentators expressed a strong dislike for the Transatlantic Trade and Investment Partnership (TTIP) with the US and the Comprehensive Economic and Trade Agreement (CETA) with Canada. The popular dissatisfaction with these free trade deals present online is in tune with offline protests as an array of diverse actors such as farmers, trade unions, small and medium-sized enterprises, and civil society organizations has fiercely opposed these free trade agreements due to a series of concerns, including the protection of labour rights, the provision of public services, and environmental standards, whose quality might putatively deteriorate as a result of the corporatization of the Euro-Atlantic economic space (see De Ville & Siles-Brugges, 2015). Throughout the comments we sampled, the role of the EU as the main negotiator of these treaties was interpreted as undemocratic, due to allegedly secretive negotiations or detrimental consequences for EU citizens' interests in terms of their rights and living conditions. The EU is viewed as a promoter of elitist interests, like those of multinational companies or financial institutions, since the negative integration that the EU has been actively propping up implies the elimination of barriers that restrict the movement of goods, services, and factors of production. These EU policies are viewed as particularly beneficial for large internationalized companies and financial entities as they obtain access to a larger market, whereas more vulnerable categories feel endangered by the increased competition stemming from an integrated market.

In terms of remedial action, or in the language of frame analysis 'prognostic' frames (see: Snow & Benford, 1988), there is an appeal to the EU to reconnect with ordinary citizens in order to prevent further disintegration:

> EU, you say you need to learn from the UK Brexit but you would never have considered change if we had voted to stay in. Now it looks as if the wheels are going to come of the bus because of the intransigence of the political elite of the EU who have no idea and are not interested in the millions of ordinary citizens throughout Europe. (Facebook page of the Commission, 29/06/2016)

This prognosis is meant to address various ills, one of which constitutes one of the main grievances–a 'diagnostic frame' that is constituted by the 'progressive impoverishment of the British working class and failed promises of European integration' to provide prosperity for all:

> Learn this: The British working class have been marginalised by subsequent British governments since Thatcher. Their living standards have been declining for over 30 years. This is the first truly proportional representation vote that they've had. They have used it to send a clear message of their dissatisfaction. The EU has not and cannot protect them from the downwards pressures on living standards, it cannot protect them from conservative government who they have never voted for. This is why they have voted out, not because their xenophobes, because they have nothing left to lose. You can blame Margaret Thatcher for destroying their industries and leaving them to rot and ruin. (Facebook page of the Commission, 29/06/2016)

Finally, the impression that reflects the post-Brexit debate is a lack of EU-enthusiasm among most of those participating in it, even those who voted to remain in the EU. This lukewarm attitude towards European integration and the perception that for many voters it was a choice 'between two evils' are illustrated by the following comment:

> Not many people love the EU here that I can see, even amongst us that voted to remain. We had two choices, leave and jump into the unknown. Stay, and head to a political future that (in my experience) even most remain voters didn't want. (Facebook page of the Commission 29/06/2016)

Discussion

The transnational sphere which this article analyses appears to be populated by mostly UK citizens anxious to address a wider audience and 'export' their debates for a wider consumption. In doing so, 'leavers' appear particularly anxious to identify and 'explain' the building blocks of Britishness, the related exceptionalism of their status of inhabitants of a proud 'island nation' that seeks to retrieve a sense of undivided identity. This finding has also been emerging from the literature, which shows how Brexit appear as a way of retrieving unity in communities that globalization had undermined (Sanadjian, 2019).

In the extensive Facebook debate that followed the unprecedented event of a member state leaving the Union, and which in small part we analysed, we have identified a number of recurring frames used to explain the Brexit vote, such as the EU democratic deficit, a diffused popular feeling of political impotence, and a large gap between EU citizens and EU elites. This chimes with frames emerging in the general Brexit debate (Hobolt, 2016). However, a surprising finding of the present analysis is the lack of the typical utilitarian and identity-based arguments that are generally utilized to support Brexit. Notwithstanding the contrasting arguments of the two blocks, in the transnational sphere we analysed only a small number of commentators supported their position on Brexit by referring to economic and migration issues, which conversely were the main topics of the general debate in the public sphere. Rather one finds recurrent concerns for the absence of EU democratic credentials, political representation within the EU system, and the remoteness of both national and EU elites from ordinary citizens. This finding speaks to the work of De Wilde et al. (2013) who examined citizens' online reactions to online news media and revealed public concerns with EU democratic legitimacy as the main driver of Euroscepticism expressed in the public debates that emerged during the 2009 European Parliament elections. Moreover, another frame that is widely used by Brexiters active on the Facebook pages of EU institutions is concern for the perceived gradual federalization of the EU, which is unfolding without a popular approval. What stems from our analysis is an overarching popular criticism that European integration has gone too far and the assertions that Europeans feel voiceless, marginalized and without the promised benefits of economic convergence and prosperity. These concerns are different from the typical concerns of security and migration because individuals interacting in the transnational sphere defined by the Facebook debate on the EU are different from the 'losers of globalization' that constituted the backbone of the Brexit vote. As has been often noted, Brexit emerged from a heterogeneous coalition not only of different social groups, but also of sometimes barely compatible cultural contents. Individuals interacting in a transnational public sphere define and cement a mini-public (For the concept of mini-public and their institutionalization see: Fung, 2003; Schmidt, 2008). The mini-public that emerged in the context of the EU-Brexiteers debate is a continuation of the long debate on EU legitimacy that took place in the context of the failed Constitutional Treaty, which was extensively articulated in the vision of a cosmopolitan ethos by its supporters, but which at the time was only cursory articulated by opponents (Statham & Trenz, 2013). We argue that Brexit constituted a political opportunity for a localist, nationalist, anti-cosmopolitan vision to emerge, to be debated and articulated by a new ideological coalition. It was then an opportunity for a principled rejection of cosmopolitanism to be aired in a transnational arena that many felt had been for too long dominated by the neo-liberal open-society vision they rejected and the EU represented. By voicing the values of nationalism, economic protectionism and cultural cohesion in a terrain of traditional EU cultural domination, the Eurosceptic commentators of this mini-public were acting as social movement activists engaged in a process of reframing.

The findings of the present analysis are in line with the stream of literature on attitudes towards European integration and perceptions of representation. They show a strong impact of perceptions of fairness of the process of decision-making on the evaluation of the EU. The majority of participants in the online fora analysed base their criticism of the EU on the argument that the EU system does not represent them and that their voices and interests are neglected by EU institutions, which are mostly perceived as self-serving bodies, or bodies that are solely promoting the interest of financial institutions and businesses. The salience of the EU's democratic deficit, as the main diagnostic frame of the Brexit vote, demonstrates a divergence between the discourse of ordinary British citizens discussing Brexit online, who criticized the EU as utterly undemocratic, and the discourses of the media and political elites, which focused mainly on EU policies regarding internal and external migration.

To sum up, first, the 'people versus elites' cleavage has proved to be the overarching frame of the post-Brexit vote Facebook debate unfolding on the pages of EU institutions. This finding speaks to the scholarly literature that identifies a strong populist ethos in the Brexit process. As a number of scholars argue, the referendum empowered those 'left behind' by globalization and Europeanisation (Ford & Goodwin, 2014) and offered them an opportunity to express their discontent with national and EU elites and have the final say on the future of the UK's membership in the EU. The anti-elitist character of the Brexit vote crosses the left-right divide. It is reflected in the fact that sizeable numbers of both Conservative and Labour voters chose the Leave option, whilst the majority of UK political elites supported EU membership. In European politics, the Brexit debate was not the first instance of citizens' anti-elitist stand. For instance, the 2005 referendums in France and the Netherlands also reflected a gap between political and social elites and the general electorate (Crum, 2007).

As noted anti-establishment sentiments in relation to economic deprivation and cultural estrangement are not a distinctive feature of British politics. They are a broader phenomenon that has been connected to the recent success of a wide number of radical right populist parties (Norris, 2005; Akkerman, Mudde, & Zaslove, 2014). In addition, supply-side political dynamics have been connected to anti-system sentiments (Ruzza, 2017). This includes the transformation of party systems and the emergence of cartel parties, which heavily rely on state resources in contexts of low levels of popular trust (Hino, 2012). Furthermore, the securitization of migration issues and the porosity of national economies in the situation of global economic and financial interdependence have facilitated the emergence of populist parties, which are advocating the repatriation of national powers from Brussels and the erection of physical or figurative walls to address an emerging need for social protection (Ruzza, 2017 (forthcoming)). The Leave side managed to successfully articulate these fears.

Secondly, it has been argued that the ideological contents expressed by participants in the transnational sphere identified differ from those typically emerged in the public sphere in the run up to the referendum and during its immediate aftermaths. The reasons for this difference is attributed to the specific features, ideological concerns and political culture of the mini-public defined by individuals able and willing to access a transnational debate on EU institutions.

Disclosure statement

No potential conflict of interest was reported by the authors.

ORCID

Carlo Ruzza ⓘ http://orcid.org/0000-0002-4003-477X

References

Aichholzer, G., & Strauß, S. (2016). *Electronic participation in Europe* (pp. 55–132). New York, USA: Electronic Democracy in Europe: Prospects and Challenges of E-Publics, E-Participation and E-Voting: Springer.

Akkerman, A., Mudde, C., & Zaslove, A. (2014). How populist are the people? Measuring populist attitudes in voters. *Comparative Political Studies*, *47*(9), 1324–1353.

Baker, D., Gamble, A., Randall, N. J., & Seawright, D. (2008). Euroscepticism in the British party system: 'A source of fascination, perplexity, and sometimes frustration'. In P. Taggart & A. Szczerbiak (Eds.), *Opposing Europe? The comparative party politics of Euroscepticism* (pp. 93–116). Oxford, UK: Oxford University Press.

Balch, A., & Balabanova, E. (2017). A deadly cocktail? The fusion of Europe and immigration in the UK press. *Critical Discourse Studies*, *14*(3), 236–255.

Barberá, P., Vaccari, C., & Valeriani, A. (2017). Social media, personalisation of news reporting, and media systems' polarisation in Europe. In M. Barisione & A. Michailidou (Eds.), *Social media and European politics. Rethinking power and legitimacy in the digital era* (pp. 25–52). London: Palgrave MacMillan.

Barisione, M., & Ceron, A. (2017). A digital movement of opinion? Contesting austerity through social media. In M. Barisione & A. Michailidou (Eds.), *Social media and European politics. Rethinking power and legitimacy in the digital era* (pp. 77–104). London: Palgrave MacMillan.

Beciu, C., Mădroane, I. D., Cârlan, A. I., & Ciocea, M. (2017). Power relations, agency and discourse in transnational social fields. *Critical Discourse Studies*, *14*(3), 227–235.

Bossetta, M., Segestean, A. D., & Trenz, H.-J. (2017). Transnational citizen engagement through social media: The factual, the ideological, and the moral style. In M. Barisione & A. Michailidou (Eds.),

Social media and European politics. Rethinking power and legitimacy in the digital era (pp. 53–76). London: Palgrave MacMillan.

Carey, S., & Burton, J. (2004). The influence of the press in shaping public opinion towards the European Union in Britain. *Political Studies, 52*(3), 623–640.

Cheneval, F., & Nicolaidis, K. (2017). The social construction of demoicracy in the European Union. *European Journal of Political Theory, 16*(2), 235–260.

Clarke, J., & Newman, J. (2017). 'People in this country have had enough of experts': Brexit and the paradoxes of populism. *Critical Policy Studies, 11*(1), 101–116.

Cornelissen, J. P., & Werner, M. D. (2014). Putting framing in perspective: A review of framing and frame analysis across the management and organizational literature. *Academy of Management Annals, 8*(1), 181–235.

Crum, B. (2007). Party stances in the referendums on the EU constitution. *European Union Politics, 8*(1), 61–82.

Curry, A. (2017). The city, the country, and the new politics of place. *Journal of Futures Studies, 21*(3), 1–14.

Daddow, O. (2012). The UK media and 'Europe': From permissive consensus to destructive dissent. *International Affairs, 88*(6), 1219–1236.

Daddow, O. (2013). Margaret Thatcher, Tony Blair and the Eurosceptic tradition in Britain. *The British Journal of Politics and International Relations, 15*(2), 210–227.

Del Vicario, M., Zollo, F., Caldarelli, G., Scala, A., & Quattrociocchi, W. (2017). Mapping social dynamics on Facebook: The Brexit debate. *Social Networks, 50*, 6–16.

De Ville, F., & Siles-Brugges, G. (2015). *TTIP: The truth about the transatlantic trade and investment partnership*. Cambridge, UK: Polity.

De Wilde, P., Michailidou, A., & Trenz, H.-J. (2013). *Contesting Europe. Exploring Euroscepticism in online media coverage*. Colchester: ECPR Press.

Diez Medrano, J. (2003). *Framing Europe: Attitudes to European integration in Germany, Spain, and the United Kingdom*. Princeton: Princeton University Press.

European Commission-Directorate General Communication, & Gallup Organization. (2011). *Flash Eurobarometer 318: Attitudes towards the EU in the United Kingdom*.

Fernández, J. J., Eigmüller, M., & Börner, S. (2016). Domestic transnationalism and the formation of pro-European sentiments. *European Union Politics, 17*(3), 457–481.

Ford, M., & Goodwin, M. (2014). *Revolt on the right: Explaining support for the radical right in Britain*. Abingdon: Routledge.

Forster, A. (2002). *Euroscepticism in British politics*. New York: Routledge.

Freeden, M. (2017). After the Brexit referendum: Revisiting populism as an ideology. *Journal of Political Ideologies, 22*(1), 1–11.

Fung, A. (2003). Survey article: Recipes for public spheres: Eight institutional design choices and their consequences. *Journal of Political Philosophy, 11*(3), 338–367.

George, S. (1990). *An awkward partner: Britain in the European community*. Oxford: Oxford University Press.

Grant, C. (2008). *Why is Britain Eurosceptic?* London, UK: Centre for European Reform.

Hino, A. (2012). *New challenger parties in Western Europe: A comparative analysis*. London: Routledge.

Hobolt, S. B. (2016). The Brexit vote: A divided nation, a divided continent. *Journal of European Public Policy, 23*(9), 1259–1277.

Inglehart, R. F., & Norris, P. (2016). *Trump, Brexit, and the rise of populism: Economic have-nots and cultural backlash*. Cambridge, MA: Kennedy School of Government, Harvard University, Faculty Research Working Paper Series.

Krzyżanowski, M. (2015). International leadership re-/constructed? On the ambivalence and heterogeneity of identity discourses in European Union policy on climate change. *Journal of Language and Politics, 14*(1), 110–133.

Krzyzanowski, M. (2018). Social media in/and the politics of the European Union: Politico-organizational communication, institutional cultures and self-inflicted elitism. *Journal of Language and Politics, 17* (1), 1–24.

McEvoy, C. (2016). The role of political efficacy on public opinion in the European Union. *JCMS: Journal of Common Market Studies*, *54*(5), 1159–1174.

Michailidou, A. (2017). Twitter, public engagement and the Eurocrisis: More than an echo Chamber? In M. Barisione & A. Michailidou (Eds.), *Social media and European politics. Rethinking power and legitimacy in the digital era* (pp. 241–266). London: Palgrave MacMillan.

Michailidou, A., & Trenz, H. J. (2013). Mediatized representative politics in the European Union: Towards audience democracy? *Journal of European Public Policy*, *20*(2), 260–277.

Michailidou, A., & Trenz, H. J. (2015). The European crisis and the media: Media autonomy, public perceptions and new forms of political engagement. In H. J. Trenz, C. Ruzza, & V. Guiraudon (Eds.), *Europe in Crisis: The unmaking of political union* (pp. 232–250). London: Palgrave MacMillan.

Monforte, P. (2014). The cognitive dimension of social movements' Europeanization processes. The case of the protests against 'fortress Europe'. *Perspectives on European Politics and Society*, *15*(1), 120–137.

Norris, P. (2005). *Radical right: Voters and parties in the electoral market*. Cambridge: Cambridge University Press.

Rohrschneider, R. (2002). The democracy deficit and mass support for an EU-wide government. *American Journal of Political Science*, *46*(2), 463–475.

Ruzza, C., & Bozzini, E. (2006). Anti-Americanism and the European peace movement: The Iraq war. In S. Fabbrini (Eds.), *The United States contested: American unilateralism and European discontent* (pp. 112–129). London: Routledge.

Ruzza, C. (2006). Frame analysis. In K. Brown (Ed.), *Encyclopedia of language and linguistics* (pp. 3214–3221). Oxford: Elsevier.

Ruzza, C. (2017). Populism and political movements. In C. Holtz-Bacha, O. Mazzoleni, & R. Heinisch (Eds.), *Handbook on political populism* (pp. 87–103). Baden-Baden: Nomos Verlag.

Sanadjian, M. (2019). Identification, the exercise of democracy and the fear of the other – the June EU referendum in the UK. *Social Identities*, *25*(2), 110–124.

Schmidt, V. A. (2008). Discursive institutionalism: The explanatory power of ideas and discourse. *Annual Review of Political Science*, *11*(1), 303–326.

Snow, D. A., & Benford, R. D. (1988). Ideology, frame resonance, and participant mobilization. *From Structure to Action: Comparing Social Movement Research Across Cultures International Social Movement Research*, *1*, 197–217.

Statham, P., & Trenz, H. J. (2013). How European Union politicization can emerge through contestation: The constitution case. *JCMS: Journal of Common Market Studies*, *51*(5), 965–980.

Tarţa, A.-G. (2017). A framework for evaluating European social media publics: The case of the European Parliament's Facebook page. In M. Barisione & A. Michailidou (Eds.), *Social media and European politics. Rethinking power and legitimacy in the digital era* (pp. 143–165). London: Palgrave MacMillan.

Vicari, S. (2010). Measuring collective action frames: A linguistic approach to frame analysis. *Poetics*, *38*(5), 504–525.

'Crisis' as a discursive strategy in Brexit referendum campaigns

Samuel Bennett

ABSTRACT

The EU referendum was arguably the greatest political event in British politics since 1945 and the campaign was marked by divisive rhetoric. This paper investigates how Britain's membership of Europe was narrated as a crisis by both sides of the discussion. I claim that this was a conscious discursive strategy by campaign actors for two reasons. Firstly, by constructing an event as a crisis implies that immediate measures need to be taken (by voters) to correct the situation. Secondly, this discursive strategy allowed actors from Leave and Remain campaigns to suspend partisan political divisions which would normally compromise co-operation. The chosen site of analysis is the televised EU referendum debate, entitled 'The Great Debate', which was broadcast two days before the referendum of June 23rd 2016.

1. A discursive 'crisis' of EU membership

Crises do not exist outside of their social construction; they are brought into existence and resolved through communication (Hearit & Courtright, 2003). *It is not just how a crisis event is narrated, but how an event is narrated as a crisis*. Crises, according to Falkheimer and Heide (2010, p. 514) are social, political and cultural phenomena: 'a crisis is a crisis due to the fact that different groups, interested parties and institutions perceive and experience it as crisis'. Indeed, we can speak of 'crisis discourses' (Krzyżanowska & Krzyżanowski, 2018, p. 613) that 'come together' with other discourses, e.g. of Europe, the economy, or Immigration. In crisis events understandings of symbolic 'objects of reference (such as Europe or the nation-state) are contested, negotiated, reformulated and reorganized' (Krzyżanowski, Triandafyllidou, & Wodak, 2009a, p. 5). Via practices of recontextualisation, discourses of, for example the nation-state, are 'under continuous negotiation and re-negotiation' (Stråth, 2000, p. 14). According to Stråth and Wodak (2009, p. 16), crisis are often narrated through appeals to specific values. More specifically, 'various values are violated (e.g. values of 'freedom', 'human rights' etc.) while different actors use those crises to express (in/through the media) their defence of different values … in order to thus legitimise their viewpoints/ideas on the changing social, political and economic order' (Krzyżanowski, 2009, p. 20). Some of these values are constructed as universal, others are constructed as national-or regional- context specific, i.e. 'European values' (Triandafyllidou,

Wodak, & Krzyżanowski, 2009) or 'British values' (Bennett, 2018) and research has shown that values are differently interpreted depending on country context (Krzyżanowski, Triandafyllidou, & Wodak, 2009b).

In such narrations of social phenomena, the future is often seen as negative, which in turn demands that action be taken now to rectify the situation (Dunmire, 2005). By extending a crisis 'into an indeterminate future' (Dunmire, 2005, p. 507), 'political evocations tap into – indeed prey upon – the public's general anxiety about the inherent ambiguity and indeterminacy of the future in order to influence social perceptions, cognitions, and actions' (Dunmire, 2005, p. 484). Actors will try to discursively and strategically construct a crisis as inevitable unless action is taken, but in reality these events are shaped and come into being through talk and text (De Rycker & Don, 2013). Thus, constructing an event as a crisis has obvious persuasive appeal. It can be used to exhort people to act (politicians to divert resources, people to vote or participate in other social action such as demonstrations or vigilantism).

The UK referendum on whether to leave or remain in the European Union was probably the greatest political event in British politics since 1945. The final result, 52% of the electorate voting to leave, was not predicted and the campaign was marked by extremely strong rhetoric on both sides, especially by the unofficial 'leave' campaign led by Nigel Farage (Bennett, 2019a), which culminated in the infamous 'Breaking Point' poster. Like many referendum campaigns (Atikcan, 2018; Petithomme, 2011), it was marked by a suspension of partisan politics, with both sides engaging in cross-party cooperation. The vote was narrated by many on both sides of the divide as a crisis point: As a decision that would either precipitate a crisis or resolve an on-going one. In this paper I claim that this was a conscious discursive strategy on the part of campaign actors. As argued above, by constructing an event as a crisis implies that corrective measures need to be taken. More importantly, though, the focus on UK membership of the EU as a crisis allowed actors from the Leave and Remain campaigns to suspend political partisan divisions. That is, they moved the discussion 'above' politics, the plane of – at times existential – crisis in order to bypass the partisan contradictions and lack of ideological cohesion in their campaigns. To explain how this occurred through discursive action, I analyse the 'Great Debate', televised on BBC1 two days before the referendum. The structure of the paper is as follows: following an explanation of historical and present-day splits in political attitudes towards EU membership in the UK, I move to theoretical considerations of the nature of EU referendum voting and campaigns. Next comes section on the form and function of televised campaign debates, after which I present the analysis in which I identify three different crises in the discourse: temporal, inter-discursive, and ideological, the last of which brings to light how latent partisan cleavages can still (re)materialise, and be consciously deployed, within a referendum campaign.

2. Standing on a precipice: historical fissures and a crisis of discourse

Britain's relationship – both its public and political elite – with the various iterations of the European Union can be described as, at best, ambivalent (cf. Bennett, 2019a). On a public level a prominent Euro-sceptic streak has existed that runs through the 'national mind-set' (Kenealy, 2016) since Britain joined the EEC after a referendum in 1974. At the political level, leaders of the Conservative and Labour parties have been supportive of EU membership, albeit often whilst having quite confrontational approaches to negotiations (e.g. when Margaret Thatcher called for a UK rebate in the 1980s) or wanting to negotiate special dispensation, as David Cameron did before ultimately calling the referendum.

At the same time though, both political parties have had to deal with internal rebellion from Euro-sceptic MPs and party members and Europe has played a big part in termination of the last three Conservative Prime Ministers' tenures. Ideologically, the issue of Britain in Europe has been historically problematic for the major parties. To begin with, the single market appealed to the free-market principles of many Conservatives (Bennett, 2019b), but as EU integration deepened, Thatcher faced back-bench rebellion against entry into the Exchange Rate Mechanism (a step towards a single currency) and later, John Major faced considerable party backlash for signing the Maastricht Treaty in 1992 as it was seen as undermining 'the British tradition of inviolable sovereignty of Parliament' (Kenealy, 2016), a topic that would also play a large part in the 'Leave' campaign for the 2016 referendum. For Labour, the issue has been the protection of workers from the machinations of a free market, especially to protect jobs. Thus on immigration, Labour leaders have often found themselves faced with internal criticism (Bennett, 2019b). On the one hand, Europe provides a platform for cross-national solidarity and the protection of workers' rights; this was the Europe trumpeted by Tony Blair, signified by his signature of European Convention on Human Rights. On the other, historically those on the left of the party (from former leaders such as High Gaitskill and Michel Foot to the current leader, Jeremy Corbyn) have seen European membership as a threat to workers and social-ist policies and have campaigned against its free-market, neo-liberal tendencies. Again this trend was clear in Corbyn's role in the 'Remain' campaign, with some on the left of the party criticising him for 'white-washing' his historical Euro-sceptic views and pro-EU Labour members questioning the relatively low profile he took during the campaign (BBC News, 2016).

The EU referendum came about due to two key (yet highly complex) political processes. The first was the increasing Euro-scepticism in the Conservative party after the 2008 Euro crisis. As the EU moved towards deeper integration of banking and finance, the Euro-sceptic wing of the party became ever-more vocal, using Parliament and access to a Euro-sceptic media to decry the end goal of a federal Europe. The second was the rise of the United Kingdom Independence Party (UKIP) under the leadership of Nigel Farage.[1] This rise has in part been blamed on a 'mutiny within conservatism' (Parris, 2014) against both Europe and Cameron's policies of 'compassionate conservatism', which traditional Conservatives saw as a betrayal of the party's ideological roots (Kelsey, 2015). UKIP's rise was also possible because it shifted from being a single issue party to a populist party, in part by discursively linking continued EU membership to other issues that were more electorally salient such as immigration, housing, and social care. Through this they could capitalise on a 'values-driven backlash among voters towards a universalistic and cosmopolitan outlook that had dominated politics and media' for almost a generation (Dennison & Goodwin, 2015, p. 185). The party was able to appeal to both 'left behind' Labour voters and disenchanted Conservatives and as such emerged as an electoral threat. To combat the electoral threat, in 2013 David Cameron stated that he would hold a referendum unless EU institutions were reformed and the 2015 Conservative election manifesto included a similar pledge.

Unlike general, local, or European elections, the referendum campaigns were cross-party and there was no party whip on the issue. Thus, MPs and ministers from both major parties were split between leave and remain. The official Remain Campaign was led by Britain Stronger in Europe, which Cameron and Corbyn campaigned for, although Corbyn refused throughout the period to appear at events with Conservative MPs. The official leave campaign group was known as 'Vote Leave' and again had cross-party support, including well-known Labour MPs such as Gisela Stuart and prominent Conservative ministers (e.g. Boris Johnson and Michael Gove) who were able to capture the attention of, and at times, pen article for, the Euro-sceptic press. Two other leave groups were also influential: Leave. EU, funded by the UKIP backer Aaron Banks, and 'Grassroots out', which emerged after infighting in the other two groups and included Nigel Farage, Kate Hoey (Labour) and Liam Fox (Conservatives). As well as cross-party groups, there were also party-internal groups campaigning for both sides, additionally highlighting the atypical, non-partisan nature of the referendum campaign.

Whilst there is limited space here to review the whole campaign, it is worth briefly mentioning that the rhetoric employed by campaigners were roundly criticised at the time. Remain were claimed to have run a highly negative campaign that pointed to the feared costs of leaving, dubbed 'project fear', whilst the official Leave campaign were condemned for overstating the impact that the EU had on British politics and the cost of continued membership. On top of this, Farage was criticised for his strong anti-immigration stance.

3. Brexit: (not) just another European referendum

Over recent years there has been a general shift to a more issue-based form of politics and more emphasis on alternative forms of political action (Schmitt-Beck & Farrell, 2002a). Together, this has led to an increasing importance of political campaigns, in for example, referendums, which offer citizens a more direct possibility to be politically active. One area in which referendums have frequently occurred is in relation to the European Union. Whilst the EU does not require referendums on membership or ratification of treaties, many states have done so (especially regarding membership) and some either have this inscribed in national law (i.e. Ireland) or have been forced to call referendums after legal judgements (France in 2005). There has been a total of forty-eight referendums held by EU members or candidate countries, forty of which have been held since 1992. They fall roughly into two types (McCormick, 2014, p. 214): those on membership (joining, leaving, adoption of the Euro) and those on single issues. The latter includes ratifying treaties (Maastricht 1992, Amsterdam 1998, Nice 2001, Lisbon 2008), the European Constitution (2005), financial bail-outs (Greece 2015), opt-outs from EU regulations (Denmark 2015), and accepting EU-set migrant quotas (Hungary 2016). The first negative vote in an EU referendum came in the form of Denmark's rejection of the Maastricht Treaty, which, according to McCormick (2014, p. 214), marked the end of the long-standing 'permissive consensus' towards European institutions and integration. Since then, there have been ever more referendums and ever more negative votes, culminating in the UK referendum to leave the EU in 2016.

Theories accounting for voting decisions in (European) elections and referendums can be divided into two main types. The first set contends that voters' decisions are rooted in their broad attitudes to Europe (e.g. Carey, 2002). Those with a strong sense of European identity are 'inclined to embrace the European Union as a symbolic representation of that identity' (Curtice, 2017, p. 20), whereas those with a strong sense of nationally-grounded identity are more likely to see the EU and any further integration as a threat. Others (cf. Garry, Marsh, & Sinnott, 2005; McLaren, 2004) claim that voting is based on instrumental – predominantly economic – self-interest; those economically better positioned to take advantage of the EU (labour mobility, education, travel) are more likely to have a positive attitude. Another sub-set of this theoretical approach is found in claims that the electorate cast their votes based on their attitude towards the (EU) issue at hand (cf. Ehin, 2001).

By contrast, the second theoretical approach tries to understand referendum results as reflections of (dis)satisfaction with domestic politics (Atikcan, 2018; see also Anderson, 1998; Armingeon & Ceka, 2014; Reif & Schmitt, 1980). Curtice (2017, p. 20) calls these 'proxy measures' and include attitudes towards the incumbent government (a chance to give the government a 'bloody nose') or the state of democracy at home. Alternatively, due to a lack of interest, sense of affiliation, or knowledge, they may take supplement their knowledge with other people's cues (Curtice, 2017).

It is this final point that is important within the framework of this paper. Research in the form of Eurobarometer (cf. McCormick, 2014) has shown a 'knowledge deficit' exists throughout EU citizens on how it functions and affects day-to-day lived experiences. As McCormick (2014, p. 212) argues there exists 'a gap between the process of European integration and the ability of EU voters to make reasonably informed judgements about that process'. As a result, voters rely on 'cues' (Curtice, 2017, p. 21) or 'information shortcuts' (McCormick, 2014, p. 213) when in the voting booth. There is instead a reliance on elite actors, not least partisan politicians and the media. This knowledge deficit, argues McCormick (2014, p. 217) is open to manipulation and the use of discursive strategies based on 'fear, misinformation and selective use of facts' in order to 'state their case and to characterise the opportunities and threats inherent in integration'. Dinan (2012, p. 95) for example, claims that EU referendums are 'lightning rods for Euro-sceptics … because they can easily manipulate them'. There can be attempts to inculcate a sense of crisis (be it economic, identity, demographic, or moral). For example, in the June 2008 referendum in Ireland on the Lisbon Treaty the 'No' side played up the risk of EU law meaning the end of a ban on abortion.

If we accept there is a knowledge deficit on Europe and that this gap is filled at least in part by elite actors (politicians and media), then it is paramount that the information provided to voters in referendum campaigns be analysed in order to understand how certain domestic and European issues become salient (Atikcan, 2018, p. 93). Likewise, Schmitt-Beck and Farrell (2002b, p. 186) argue that 'the rhetorical activity undertaken by political actors in order to improve their electoral prospects seem to matter to voters'. It is also important to identify key actors and how they rely on or bypass traditional political cleavages, as well as their presence in campaigns and how they are depicted in the media (De Vreese & Semetko, 2004).

European referendums 'temporarily displace traditional party cleavages' (Petithomme, 2011, p. 90) and this can affect the potency of respective Yes/No, In/out campaigns. Often there is 'de facto collusion' (Petithomme, 2011) between the main governing and opposition parties; ideological support will trump strategic, partisan opposition – often only just – and this will lead to intra-party dissent because of a lack of ideological cohesion inherent in these temporary co-operations. This is especially the case for mainstream opposition parties, but is also problematic for governing parties (Petithomme, 2011). For De Vreese and Semetko (2004), strategic political alliances can affect the sharpness and coherences of a referendum campaign, as was the case with Brexit. To say that Labour under Corbyn and Cameron's Conservatives were uncomfortable campaign bedfellows for Remain would be an understatement, even on purely ideological terms and there was an additional reticence by both parties to appear on united platforms because of impending local and mayoral elections (Curtice, 2017). Furthermore, Labour was not active in communicating their stance on the referendum and when they were, it was reported either negatively or neutrally by a largely Euro-sceptic press (Curtice, 2017).

In EU referendum campaigns the pro-European 'cartel' (Petithomme, 2011, p. 90) consisting of main parties can also be a clarion call for otherwise peripheral political actors and parties, who can prove pivotal in referendum campaigns, especially if they have 'captured' the issue (as UKIP during Brexit, see above). When mainstream parties unite, it can be framed by populist political actors as 'the people vs. the establishment' (cf. Bennett, 2019b), with the EU being yet another layer of establishment. For example, according to LeDuc (2002, p. 153) during the French referendum on the Maastricht Treaty the No camp were politically varied, but they were able to 'portray themselves as political outsiders' and from here 'captured the mood of disenchantment with the political class at the time'. In the UK, it is arguable that Brexit was also, at least in some small part, the result of similar disenchantment with traditional political actors ('lies' over Iraq, the MPs' expenses scandal, the financial crisis etc.).

Thus, following Petithomme (2011) if mainstream opposition parties are unreliable and periphery parties have mobilised, then the outcome of EU referendums are linked to the engagement of the governing party. However, as mentioned above, whilst this has often been enough for the Yes camp to get over the line in referendums throughout the Union, in the case of Brexit, the governing party (both MPs and 'lay' members) was also ideologically split. Furthermore, so-called 'big hitters' within the party with strong media presences, such as Boris Johnson and Michael Gove, campaigned to leave. Overall, traditional party cues (from party leaders) did not work. Only 37% of traditional Conservative voters followed Cameron's call to remain, whilst 64% of Labour supporters followed Corbyn (Curtice, 2017, p. 33). Indeed, voters who would normally back opposition parties were more likely to support the government's position than government supporters were (Curtice, 2017).

Atikcan (2018, p. 93) contends that in EU referendums the anti-EU side often has agenda control of the campaign and that there is an 'asymmetrical political advantage' for No campaigners because they boost fears by (inter)discursively linking the referendum to less popular issues. In this theory, the broader the topic of the referendum, the better No are placed and there is more space to 'attack' on multiple fronts (Atikcan, 2018, 96). This might be conceived of as issue capture, or issue broadening (De Vreese & Semetko, 2004). Conversely, if the referendum is on a single issue or if, the referendum issue is limited after EU concessions (after initially negative referendum results) then the advantage is with the pro-European side. Thus, the Leave campaign in Brexit were able to, as it were, stretch an already broad issue to encompass other (domestic) crises of, for example immigration, housing, school places, health access etc. Historically, No campaigns often argue about loss of autonomy, citizenship or moral issues, even when treaties don't include these topics and when they are successful in changing the frame of the debate, this can lead to a rejection of European integration, for example Denmark's vote to join the Euro in 1999. Additionally, there does not have to be any ideological cohesion to the No/Leave critique of the EU, they need only 'to raise doubts or link the proposal to other less popular issues' (Atikcan, 2018, p. 96). During the UK referendum, and in the years running up to it, UKIP had been able to capture the issue of Europe by discursively linking it to immigration (Bennett, 2019b). The Leave camp ran an aggressive campaign which put Remain on the defensive and so it was hard to reframe the debate and get their key message on the economic costs of leaving across. So, while Yes camps have been found to generally have an advantage when a referendum campaign has centred on economic costs or benefits (Atikcan, 2018, p. 93), this was not the case for Remain during the UK referendum. Leave managed to successfully challenge the economic claims through a combination of misinformation and anti-establishment rhetoric against specialists, with Michael Gove claiming that 'the people of this country have had enough of experts from organisations with acronyms saying that they know best and getting it consistently wrong' (Sky News, 2016).

Concluding this theoretical section I see three key, connected points that need to be highlighted. Firstly, the Brexit referendum campaigns of Leave and Remain did not herald in a new post-partisan era British politics. Whilst there was a strategic, pragmatic, and possibly cognitive suspension of traditional alignment and bracketing of political identities, ideological and partisan cleavages still remained; actors refused to share platforms and even in debates, party identities were invoked as a rhetorical strategy. Secondly, both sides resorted to crisis frames. On the one hand this served to shift the debate above and beyond politics to more 'vital', existential issues (e.g. sovereignty). On the other, this also allowed them to overcome and background deep ideological and partisan splits that would otherwise prove problematic in electoral campaigning. This was a reversal of Benjamin Disraeli's oft-quoted adage 'damn your principles, stick to your party' and for the period of the Brexit campaign at least it was more a case of 'damn your party, stick to your principles'. Thirdly, as argued above, this strategy was easier – and more successful – for 'Leave', who were able to make the debate multi-dimensional, and framed it around issues which they had gained ownership of in the public sphere. These issues were more suited to crisis frames and were linked to other pre-existing events and processes that had already successfully been discursively constructed and narrated as crises, and which had become increasingly politically salient.

4. Televised political debates

4.1. Form and function

In the UK the first televised debate was held in 2010 and debates have subsequently been held for the 2015 and 2017 general elections,[2] as well as elections in Scotland, Wales and Northern Ireland. There appears to be no existing research on televised referendum debates, possibly because in comparison to elections they happen much less frequently. As mentioned in the previous section, referendum campaigns, and by extension, televised debates, differ in nature to those for elections, primarily because party affiliation is suspended and so actors don't have recourse to traditional partisan modes of political attack based on ideological lines. That said, such debates share the same two main functional goals: influencing voting behaviour and filling knowledge gaps. Debates offer the chance to present a lot of information to viewers that is not recontextualised by media outlets who increasingly insert their voices into reports (Benoit & Benoit-Bryan, 2013).

In the UK televised debates form part of a wider trend towards an Americanisation of political action, including 'a greater focus on the party leader and candidate personality; the growing use of marketing-derived research methods; the proliferation of specialist political consultants; and an increased role for communication technology, especially broadcast media, and latterly, the internet' (Anstead, 2016). TV debates can be seen as a form 'confrontainment' (Luginbühl, 2007, p. 1371) in which politics revolves around personalities via mediated performance (Drake & Higgins, 2012) and whilst they include elements of discussion and political argument, a key part of this is the performance of authenticity (Drake & Higgins, 2012). Whilst party leaders have become celebrities (or at least are expected to act like they are), they operate in a system where power relies on gaining a parliamentary majority in which co-operation is required to pass legislation, albeit maintaining party allegiances and promoting party manifestoes. As a sub-genre of political discourse, they are also unique in their participatory nature. During the debate there is a 'complex network of address' in play, which includes a debate mediator, opponent(s), allies, studio audience, TV audience and the media (Drake & Higgins, 2012, p. 380). They are thus marked by 'doubly articulated' forms of address: Most of the time, the communicative interaction in debates is between those actively participating, but they are 'designed to be heard by absent audiences' (Scannell, 1991, p. 1).

4.2. The 2016 EU referendum debate

The televised EU referendum debate analysed below, entitled 'The Great Debate' was broadcast live on BBC1 on 21st June 2016, two days before the referendum. It was the largest of a number of televised debates throughout the campaigning period and was the first time that the TV debate format had been used nationally for a non-parliamentary election.[3] It was held at Wembley Arena in front of a studio audience of approximately 6,000 people and 3.8 m viewers.

The debate differed in two key ways from typical 'presidential' style ones. Firstly, participants were not representing political parties and as a result, so as far as possible they had to bracket their party affiliations and instead share a platform with people who were from different parties but who were supporting one of the two referendum options (Leave or Remain). This has an impact on potential data because the participants were there to represent a policy option, not an overtly ideological party position, the character of the debate would likely be less based on attacks on past government decisions and affiliation. That is, the speakers would not be able to fall back on the traditional repertoire of discursive strategies and frames based on party politics and political ideologies and would thus have to find other means to persuade viewers to vote one way or another.

In total the programme was two hours long in total and transcript ran to 17.5k words. In the main portion of the debate, after a general introduction, each side nominated one person to give a brief opening speech. Each side was represented by three participants. The 'Leave' side consisted of Boris Johnson (Conservative and former Mayor of London), Gisela Stuart (Labour) and Andrea Leadsom (Conservative and then-Energy Minister).

The 'Remain' side was made up of Sadiq Khan (Labour and Mayor of London), Ruth Davidson (Conservative and leader of the Conservatives in the Scottish Parliament) and Frances O'Grady (Secretary General of the Trades Union Congress). The debate was split into three thematic sections ('Immigration', 'The Economy', and 'Britain's Place in the World') each of which were preceded by a video that showed facts and figures and key arguments for each side. At the end of the main debate there were closing statements from each side.[4]

5. Analysis[5]

5.1. Brexit as a crisis point

Temporally, the referendum was narrated as a crisis point, a turning point, whereby change could be made. For 'Leave' speakers the crisis was already present and the solution was leaving the EU, in this discursive strategy, one constant refrain was the topos of control.

> (1) *If we vote leave and take back control, I believe that this Thursday can be our country's independence day* (BJ-L)

> (2) *I am told you can't do this, you can't do that because of the EU. There are five presidents of the EU. Can anyone name them? And can anyone vote for them? You don't vote for them because you are not allowed to vote for them and you can't kick them out either* (AL-L)

In excerpt 1 the future is foregrounded as (potentially) bringing a key benefit through the second conditional and the use of the hyperbolic 'Independence Day', which represents the symbolic importance of sovereignty and implies that the country is being controlled outside forces. It is a positive appeal to consequences. The coherence of the entire claim relies on two presuppositions: Firstly that control has been lost and secondly that the UK is not a sovereign country within the EU. Linked to sovereignty and control, in excerpt 2 Andrea Leadsom implicitly frames the problem as crisis of democracy whereby unelected people make rules that impact on everyday life. On the face of it there is no cohesion between the first of the EU stopping action and the second claim. However, cohesion is attained via the logical fallacy of *post hoc ergo propter hoc*. That is, she establishes a causal relationship between unelected representation and the inability to act as one would desire. In doing so she relies on telling the right story (Charteris-Black, 2011), in this case, the myth of a conspiratorial enemy. For cohesion be accepted, the listener must draw their own conclusions between the two statements. Furthermore, by using rhetorical questions, she situates the audience as seekers of the truth and herself as the provider.

By comparison, the 'Remain' speakers often constructed the future as a potential time of crisis.

> (3) *If we come out of the EU there will be have to be border controls. Let me tell you, the way that is seen in Belfast and Derry, I really worry for our future* (FO-R)

> (4) *The big pressure on our pay and jobs wasn't to do with low-paid migrant workers. It was those greedy bankers crashing the economy, and if we leave we'll crash it again* (FO-R)

In both excerpts O'Grady engages in myth-telling and recounts two cautionary tales (Van Leeuwen, 2007). In the first, she invokes the history of the 'Troubles' in Northern

Ireland and the subsequent peace process, and in the second she recalls the 2008 financial crisis. She counterposes this with a certain, epistemic future ('will') (Dunmire, 2005), which in these cases are forms of *argumentum ad consequentiam*. By claiming there 'will have to be border controls' alternative futures are denied and a certain version of reality is privileged which can only be changed via pre-emptive action. Dunmire claims that strong modality to talk about the future can have the ideological function of denying agency and paralysing political action (2005, p. 504). However, in these cases it is used as an exhortation aimed at galvanising and persuading action (voting 'Remain' in the referendum). Her claims are enhanced by emotive language, a rhetorical tool to give her statements an increased level of pathos. In excerpt 3 she deploys the mental verb of 'worry' along with the collective 'us' to construct herself as caring about a shared future. Likewise, using a false analogy (Leaving EU is the same as the financial crisis), in (4), she places blame on 'greedy bankers' and in doing so, separates them from the positive in-group but also holds them up as an example of what will happen to the economy if the UK left the EU. A similar cautionary tale is also present in excerpt 5 as part of 'Leave's' claims.

(5) *I believe, alas, the EU is going in totally the wrong direction. It is a mistake for it to try to take on this defence component and try to evolve into a United States of Europe in the way that it is. I remember when the EU was given the task of trying to sort out the tragedy in the Balkans. You will remember what was happening in Bosnia … It was a disaster, about one million people died. It was only solved when the Americans came in.*

In response to a question about EU defence vs NATO, Johnson recounts a story about Bosnia to forewarn about a future security crisis and claim that the EU is not capable of being a federal super state (in comparison to the US). Unlike excerpts 3 and 4 though, the future crisis is left unsaid and instead the moral of the story is implied by the story itself.

5.2. An interdiscursive crisis

Another characteristic of the political discourse on the Brexit was the frequent reference to other 'crises' that were recontextualised and then interdiscursively linked to European membership.

(6) *If we have uncontrolled immigration … we will have situations like in the West Midlands where there are fifty thousand primary school places missing* (GS-L)

(7) *The bank of England has been very clear in its report, that uncontrolled immigration has had a downward pressure on wages … .Not only that, every family in this country knows how difficult it is to get the primary school place of your choice, to get a doctor's appointment and yes to afford rents or to get on to the housing ladder.* (AL-L)

(8) *The European Court has overruled British judges in being able to deport criminals. We know Ron Noble, the former head of Interpol, has said that the Schengen-free area in Europe is like hanging out a sign welcoming terrorists to Europe.* (AL-L)

In the above discourse fragments the speakers connect the EU via immigration to a number of other events and process that have also been narrated as crises, such as housing, education, and terrorism. All roads lead to Brussels: The crisis in access to symbolic public resources is caused by an immigration crisis, which itself is the result of the 'crisis' of EU membership. Through recontextualisation these other social phenomena are brought into relation with immigration and, by extension, the EU. In doing so, a discourse hierarchy is thus created so that, following Bernstein's (1990, p. 184) words, the EU 'becomes a signifier for something other than itself'. Stråth and Wodak (2009, p. 15) speak of value mobilisation in which 'experiences of crisis are mediated through appeals to specific values' which are often ideological and indications of ontological and epistemological positions. In this discursive strategy, we see Leave's attempts to stretch the referendum debate to include other issues that are not directly affected by EU membership and which are symbolically shared public goods (see also Bennett 2019b).

Digging a little deeper, the arguments used in excerpts 6 and 7 are fallacious and rely on the incorrect presupposition that immigration *is* uncontrolled, whereas in actual fact the UK does have control over its borders and could have implemented immigration further controls but decided not to because the necessary provisions (introduction of ID cards) were deemed too expensive. In 6 no supporting information is given to prove that the missing school places are due to more immigrants in the area. It also precludes other causes such as lack of government spending. Likewise in 7 the claim privileges an ideological standpoint that is based on market forces rather than on government provision. In the case of 8, Leadsom strengthens her claim via a discursive strategy of legitimisation through authority (Van Leeuwen, 2007), when she references 'the former head of Interpol'.

5.3. Brexit as an ideological crisis

The debate was generally free from overt politically ideological claims which was a result of the issue being non-partisan and members of different parties campaigning together. This notwithstanding there were hints and traces of political ideologies.

(9) *So, take back control and vote leave* (GS-L)

Perhaps the starkest ideological claim can be seen in 9 and the slogan of 'taking back control', which stands for a broader belief in the right to national and individual self-determination which have become international legal norms through, for example the UN Decolonization Declaration and the UN Universal Declaration of Human Rights). Throughout the debate the slogan was an exhortation, a call for the audience to act. It was presented as a panacea for multiple crises on the international, national and personal level, from immigration to buying a house and the 'Leave' camp placed the blame for these ills at the feet of the EU. In this sense at least, the campaign to leave was reliant on an anti-elitist, and often populist ideology. This was also visible in their questioning of experts who favoured Remain and their framing of the referendum as a chance for 'the people' to speak (Bennett, 2019b).

There were other instances when political ideologies emerged or were even foregrounded such as in 10 where Frances O'Grady (Head of the Trade Union Congress) places workers as the victims of the owners of the means of production and so clearly presents a more socialist perspective of economic relations.

(10) *Let's be honest, workers in this country have already been through a rough time. That was nothing to do with this debate. That was to do with all those bankers who crashed our economy and workers ended up paying the price* (FO-R)

As mentioned in Section 2 the Brexit campaign revealed party-political fissures and MPs had the difficult task of bracketing their every-day party identifications. However, party affiliation sometimes became visible and was actively employed in the debate as a discursive strategy.

(11) *As a conservative, and I am a proud conservative and believer in free markets, the differentials in incomes in our country have become too great ... It would be a fine thing if as Lord Rose said people on low incomes got a pay rise as a result of us taking back control of our country and our system.* (BJ-L)

In 11 Boris Johnson positively constructs himself as a conservative (through the adjective pre-modifier 'proud') but interestingly uses this as a strategy to then place him on the side of ordinary people. This is a form of pre-emptive defence against charges of being on the side of those with money and power (traditionally where a lot of Conservative support comes from) it also represents a normative view of conservatism more in line with Cameron's 'compassionate conservatism'.

(12) *Gisela, you are so wrong ... every time you and I have been in the lobby voting for bills to give workers rights, they've been in the other lobby voting against those rights* (SK-R)

Lastly, in excerpt 12 both actors are members of the Labour party and up until May 2016 both were MPs. Sadiq Khan speaks directly to Gisela Stuart and the strategy has multiple audiences. In the first, the direct recipient is his colleague Stuart, but at another level this is a political performance for the wider audience to indicate their similar views and them being on the 'right' side of the argument. This is reliant on the fallacy of false equivalence: In this instance Labour members support workers, membership of the EU protects workers and so Labour members should support the EU. I read this as a conscious discursive strategy by the speaker, not 'forgetting' of his non-partisan performance. Rather, in invoking their shared party affiliation, Khan is attacking the ideological justifications and legitimation for Stuart to be on the opposing side.

6. Conclusion

Crisis frames were employed by both sides throughout the debate. For 'Leave' participants the crisis was already present and required action to solve the crisis in form of voting to leave. Conversely, for Remain the crisis would be forthcoming unless the UK stayed within the EU. The representation of the future is an 'important component of political discourse' (Dunmire, 2005, p. 482) and responses to a crisis are shaped by contestation of crisis construal (De Rycker & Don, 2013). According to Raboy and Dagenais (1992, p. 5) 'crisis is a structuring concept: by labelling a situation as one of crisis, one declares the presence of a threat to a prevailing order'. Constructing exiting the EU as a potential crisis, as the Leave campaign did, is to imply that corrective measures are required and voters must act to save themselves and their loved ones. For 'Leave' constructing EU membership as a continuing threat 'extends the crisis into an indeterminate future' (Dunmire, 2005, p. 407) and this again exhorts action.

Secondly, EU membership was narrated as a crisis through intertextual and interdiscursive reference to other socially constructed 'crises' – immigration, sovereignty, economy and public services. As a result, a discourse hierarchy is constructed in which other discourses are appropriated and brought 'into a special relation with each other for the purpose of their selection, transmission and acquisition' (Bernstein, 1990, p. 184). The recontextualised discourse thus 'becomes a signifier for something other than itself' (Bernstein, 1990). Such an argumentation scheme is very similar to UKIP's discourse during the debate (Bennett, 2019b), and so we essentially see right-wing, exclusionary, populist discursive strategies being employed by mainstream political actors. Perceptions of events and interpretations of them as crises are, according to De Rycker and Don (2013, p. 4) 'aimed at making sense of what would otherwise be a collection of disparate and heterogeneous events'. By constructing and construing EU membership as a crisis and linking this to other 'crises' there is a 'reduction of crisis complexity' (Jessop, 2013) via 'discursive simplification' (Fairclough, 2005, p. 55). This was both a conscious discursive strategy and conscious politically strategic action; in making the referendum debate about more just EU membership, in extending it to encompass other social 'crises', Leave were able to attack on multiple fronts, allowing them to background the lack of ideological cohesion in their campaign.

The Brexit debate was constructed as a non-partisan crisis that was, I argue, placed 'above' the realm of politics. In order for this to be successful participants had to suspend their allegiances. Despite this, there were traces of ideologies, and wider world views. Many within the 'Leave' camp ran populist and anti-elitist campaigns and, to a great extent UKIP managed to set the agenda on the tone and topics of debate. Add to this is emotive language used in the campaigns and the personal attacks on participants. What we were left with was not just a discursive crisis, but a crisis of discourse.

Notes

1. See Bennett (2019b) for a detailed explanation of how UKIP managed to set the agenda in the Brexit debate and captured the issues of Europe and immigration.
2. In the latter the incumbent Prime Minister, Theresa May declined to be part of a televised debate.
3. During the Scottish referendum campaign there were two televised debates involving one representative from each side (Alex Salmond for 'Yes' and Alistair Darling for 'No').
4. After each section the discussion shifted to the secondary discussion with participants consisting of politicians, business owners, commentators and campaigners from both sides. The aim was thus to continue with the goal of persuading viewers of the merits of one position or the other and so they played an important recontextualising role in the discussion. The end of the main debate was followed by a third recontextualising 'space' for debate, backstage in the 'spin room', where a third presenter spoke to three sets of guests: BBC reporters who acted as 'fact checkers', politicians from 'Leave' and 'Remain' and journalists. For the purpose of this paper, I concentrate only on the main debate. However, further analysis of the whole programme would potentially point to patterns of discourse uptake and rejection as well as recontextualisation and other positions within the wider public discourse on the referendum.
5. Actors have been coded by initials and whether they were on the Leave (L) or Remain (R) side of the debate: Boris Johnson (BJ), Andrea Leadsom (AL), Gisela Stuart (GS), Ruth Davidson (RD), Sadiq Khan (SK), and Frances O'Grady (FO).

Acknowledgements

I would like to thank the Reviewers of the first draft of this paper for their excellent comments and suggestions on how to revise the manuscript.

Disclosure statement

No potential conflict of interest was reported by the author.

References

Anderson, C. (1998). When in doubt use proxies: Attitudes towards domestic politics and support for European integration. *Comparative Political Studies, 31*(5), 569–601.

Anstead, N. (2016). A different beast? Televised election debates in parliamentary democracies. *International Journal of Press/Politics, 21*(4), 508–526.

Armingeon, K., & Ceka, B. (2014). The loss of trust in the European Union during the great recession since 2007: The role of heuristics from the national political system. *European Union Politics, 15*(1), 82–107.

Atikcan, E. Ö. (2018). Agenda control in EU referendum campaigns: The power of the anti-EU side. *European Journal of Political Research, 57*, 93–115. doi:10.1111/1475-6765.12217

BBC. (2016, June 21). *EU referendum: The Great Debate* [TV programme]. British Broadcasting Corporation. BBC1.

BBC News. (2016, April 14). In quotes: Jeremy Corbyn and the EU referendum. *BBC News*. Retrieved from http://www.bbc.com/news/uk-politics-eu-referendum-35743994

Bennett, S. (2018). *Constructions of migrant integration in British public discourse: Becoming British*. London: Bloomsbury Academic.

Bennett, S. (2019a). Values and ideals as tools of legitimation in EU and UK Brexit discourses. In V. Koller, S. Kopf, & M. Miglbauer (Eds.), *Discourses of Brexit: Critical approaches to voices from before and after the EU referendum* (forthcoming). London: Routledge.

Bennett, S. (2019b). Standing up for 'real people': UKIP, the Brexit, and online discursive strategies on Twitter. In R. Breeze & J. Zienkowski (Eds.), *Imagining the peoples of Europe: Studies of political discourse across the ideological spectrum* (forthcoming). Amsterdam: John Benjamins.

Benoit, W., & Benoit-Bryan, J. (2013). A functional analysis of UK debates in Northern Ireland, Scotland, and Wales. *Western Journal of Communication, 78*(5), 653–667. doi:10.1080/10570314.2013.868032

Bernstein, B. (1990). *The social construction of pedagogic discourse: Vol. IV, Class, codes and control*. London: Routledge.

Carey, S. (2002). Undivided loyalties: Is national identity an obstacle to European integration? *European Union Politics, 3*(4), 387–413.

Charteris-Black, J. (2011). *Politicians and rhetoric: The persuasive power of Metaphor* (2nd ed.). Basingstoke: Palgrave Macmillan.

Curtice, J. (2017). Why leave won the UK's EU referendum. *Journal of Common Market Studies, 55*, 19–37. doi:10.1111/jcms.12613

Dennison, J., & Goodwin, M. (2015). Immigration, issue ownership and the rise of UKIP. *Parliamentary Affairs, 8*(1), 168–187.

De Rycker, A., & Don, Z. M. (2013). *Discourse and crisis: Critical perspectives*. Amsterdam: John Benjamins.

De Vreese, C., & Semetko, H. (2004). *Political campaigning in referendums: Framing the referendum issue*. Abingdon: Routledge.

Dinan, D. (2012). Governance and institutions: Impact of the escalating crisis. *Journal of Common Market Studies, 50*, 85–98.

Drake, P., & Higgins, M. (2012). Lights, camera, election: Celebrity, performance and the 2010 UK general election leadership debates. *British Journal of Politics and International Relations, 14*, 375–391.

Dunmire, P. (2005). Pre-empting the future: Rhetoric and ideology of the future in political discourse. *Discourse & Society, 16*(4), 481–513.

Ehin, P. (2001). Determinants of public support for EU membership: Data from the Baltic countries. *European Journal of Political Research, 40*(1), 31–56. doi:10.1111/1475-6765.00588

Fairclough, N. (2005). Critical discourse analysis in transdisciplinary research. In R. Wodak & P. Chilton (Eds.), *A new agenda in (critical) discourse analysis. Theory, methodology and interdisciplinarity* (pp. 53–70). Amsterdam: John Benjamins.

Falkheimer, J., & Heide, M. (2010). Crisis communicators in change: From plans to improvisations. In T. Coombs, & S. Holladay (Eds.), *Handbook of crisis communication* (pp. 511–526). Malden, MA: Wiley Blackwell.

Garry, J., Marsh, M., & Sinnott, R. (2005). 'Second-order' versus 'issue-voting' effects in EU referendums: Evidence from the Irish Nice Treaty referendums. *European Union Politics, 6*(2), 201–221.

Hearit, K., & Courtright, J. (2003). A social constructionist approach to crisis management: Allegations of sudden acceleration in the Audi 5000. *Communication Studies, 54*(1), 79–95.

Jessop, B. (2013). Recovered imaginaries, imagined recoveries: A cultural political economy of crisis construals and crisis-management in the North Atlantic financial crisis. In M. Benner (Ed.), *Before and beyond the Global economic crisis: Economics, politics and Settlement* (pp. 234–254). Cheltenham: Edward Elgar.

Kelsey, D. (2015). Hero mythology and right-wing populism: A discourse-mythological case study of Nigel Farage in the Mail Online. *Journalism Studies*. doi:10.1080/1461670X.2015.1023571

Kenealy, D. (2016, May 24). How did we get here? A brief history of Britain's Membership of the EU. *European Futures*. Retrieved from http://www.europeanfutures.ed.ac.uk/article-3278

Krzyżanowska, N., & Krzyżanowski, M. (2018). 'Crisis' and Migration in Poland: Discursive shifts, anti-pluralism and the politicisation of exclusion. *Sociology, 52*(3), 612–618. doi:10.1177/0038038518757952

Krzyżanowski, M. (2009). Europe in crisis? Discourses on crisis events in the European Press 1956-2006. *Journalism Studies, 10*(1), 18–35. doi:10.1080/14616700802560468

Krzyżanowski, M., Triandafyllidou, A., & Wodak, R. (2009a). Introduction. In A. Triandafyllidou, R. Wodak, & M. Krzyżanowski (Eds.), *European public sphere and the media: Europe in crisis* (pp. 1–12). Basingstoke: Palgrave Macmillan.

Krzyżanowski, M., Triandafyllidou, A., & Wodak, R. (2009b). Conclusions: Europe, media, crisis and the European public sphere. In A. Triandafyllidou, R. Wodak, & M. Krzyżanowski (Eds.), *European public sphere and the media: Europe in crisis* (pp. 261–268). Basingstoke: Palgrave Macmillan.

LeDuc, L. (2002). Referendums and elections: How do campaigns differ?. In D. Farrell, & R. Schmitt-Beck (Eds.), *Do political campaigns matter? Campaign effects in election and referendums* (pp. 145–162). London: Routledge.

Luginbühl, M. (2007). Conversational violence in political TV debates: Forms and functions. *Journal of Pragmatics, 39*, 1371–1387.

McCormick, J. (2014). Voting on Europe: The potential pitfalls of a British referendum. *The Political Quarterly, 85*(2), 212–219.

McLaren, L. (2004). Opposition to integration and fear of loss of national identity: Debunking a basic assumption regarding hostility to the integration project. *European Journal of Political Research, 43*(6), 895–912.

Parris, M. (2014, May 3). Ukip isn't a national party. It's a Tory sickness. *The Spectator*. Retrieved from https://www.spectator.co.uk/2014/05/ukip-isnt-a-national-party-its-a-tory-sickness/

Petithomme, M. (2011). Awakening the sleeping giant? The displacement of the partisan cleavage and change in government-opposition dynamics in EU referendums. *Perspectives on European Politics and Society, 12*(1), 89–110. doi:10.1080/15705854.2011.546149

Raboy, M., & Dagenais, B. (1992). Introduction: Media and the politics of crisis. In M. Raboy & B. Dagenais (Eds.), *Media, crisis and democracy: Mass communication and the disruption of social order* (pp. 1–15). London: Sage.

Reif, K., & Schmitt, H. (1980). Nine second-order national elections. *European Journal of Political Research, 8*(1), 3–44.

Scannell, P. (1991). *Broadcast Talk*. London: Sage.

Schmitt-Beck, R., & Farrell, D. (2002a). Studying political campaigns and their effects. In D. Farrell, & R. Schmitt-Beck (Eds.), *Do political campaigns matter? Campaign effects in election and referendums* (pp. 1–21). London: Routledge.

Schmitt-Beck, R., & Farrell, D. (2002b). Do political campaigns matter? Yes, but it depends. In D. Farrell, & R. Schmitt-Beck (Eds.), *Do political campaigns matter? Campaign effects in election and referendums* (pp. 183–193). London: Routledge.

Sky News. (2016, June 3). *Interview between Faisal Islam and Michael Gove* [TV programme]. Sky PLC.

Stråth, B. (2000). Introduction: Europe as a discourse. In B. Stråth (Ed.), *Myth and memory in the construction of community: Historical patterns in Europe and beyond* (pp. 13–44). Bivigliano: PIE-Peter Lang.

Stråth, B., & Wodak, R. (2009). Europe-discourse-politics-media-history: Constructing 'crises'? In A. Triandafyllidou, R. Wodak, & M. Krzyżanowski (Eds.), *The European public sphere and the media: Europe in crisis* (pp. 15–33). Basingstoke: Palgrave Macmillan.

Triandafyllidou, A., Wodak, R., & Krzyżanowski, M. (Eds.). (2009). *European public sphere and the media: Europe in crisis*. Basingstoke: Palgrave Macmillan.

Van Leeuwen, T. (2007). Legitimation in discourse and communication. *Discourse and Communication, 1*(1), 91–112.

Brexit and the imaginary of 'crisis': a discourse-conceptual analysis of European news media

Michał Krzyżanowski

ABSTRACT

This article explores the discourse-conceptual linkages between 'Brexit' and 'crisis' in European news media reporting about the UK referendum on leaving the European Union of 23 June 2016. The study examines media discourse about the Brexit vote in Austria, Germany, Poland and Sweden at the transformative moment in between the pre/after vote period. The conceptually-oriented critical discourse analysis shows how Brexit was not only constructed as an imaginary or a future crisis but also how its mediated visions were made real by recontextualising elements of various past social/political/economic crises. As is shown, such a strategy of discursively amalgamating the real and the imaginary, as well as the experienced/past and the expected/future, often allowed constructing Brexit as one of the most significant, critical occurrences of post-War Europe. Through the analysis, the article aims to show how wide and diverse the importance of 'Brexit as crisis' has been for European news media discourse. It also emphasises that while in the UK itself – including huge part of the UK traditional media – the critical nature of Brexit was often strategically downplayed, the wider European discourse would see it as a multifaceted 'crisis' of huge significance to both the present and the future of the EU, wider Europe and the world.

1. Introduction

'How Project Fear's dire warnings about the dangers of Brexit HAVEN'T come true two years on from the referendum' was the title of an article by Hugo Gye in the UK tabloid *The Sun* published on 27 June 2018. The article criticised Brexit opponents in the UK and wider Europe by listing several areas where it has been – according to the article incorrectly – widely predicted that Brexit would end up in crisis. The article focused specifically on issues such as, inter alia, the potential crisis of UK unemployment, increase in taxes, budget crisis of the National Health service (NHS), general national and international economic recession, or the widely discussed UK constitutional crisis. Not only did it actually disclaim all these as evidently not happening but also, typically for the UK pro-Brexit press/

media and UK right-wing populist and nationalist voices, the article generally denied as well as trivialised the rather obvious 'Brexit' and 'crisis' connection. This was done unlike in, e.g. the UK liberal quality press (e.g. the Guardian) and in the wider European and international media which widely engaged with discourses of national and pan-European socio-economic and political crisis in relation to 'Brexit'.

Departing from the above, this article aims to explore how the variety of mediated imaginaries at the 'Brexit' and 'crisis' intersection were found in the European media discourse. The paper does so in order to show that it was not only Brexit itself which has remained an evidently elusive concept – not to say an outright 'empty signifier' – but that the national as well as the international debates surrounding United Kingdom's leaving the European Union to large extent boiled down to a presentation of, and competition between, various imaginaries. Within the latter, various areas of political, social and economic reality were thematised and called into question as well as more or less explicitly linked to the future/imagined crisis caused by the UK Brexit vote and Britain's eventual departure from the EU. At the same time, as the analysis aims to show, various patterns of domestication of UK events could be observed in the European press with different types of Brexit-induced current/future crises put to the fore as a token of interpretation of the local/national impact of the largely-unexpected UK 2016 referendum results.

The article explores European news media discourse about Brexit at the time of, and immediately after, the UK Brexit referendum of 23 June 2016. It specifically looks at the transformative moment in between the pre/after vote period in order to capture the wide array of international crisis imaginaries often rooted in scenarios of future course of actions and events. At the centre of the analysis here is the critical discourse analysis of media in selected 'prototypical' EU countries including, in alphabetical order, Austria, Germany, Poland and Sweden. Hence, the paper looks at discourses in countries characterised by significantly varied length of EU membership, by different relationships with the 'core' EU project and by differentiated levels of social, political and economic ties to the UK. The focus is on how such a sample of national press in the studied countries covered Brexit and, in particular, what were their interpretations thereof immediately after the pro-Brexit results of the UK 2016 referendum came to be known.

This study joins the existent body of analyses of Brexit as a populist and nationalist project (Evans & Menon, 2017; O'Toole, 2018) as well as the growing body of work on UK and international media and political conceptualisations of, and discourses about, Brexit (see articles in this Special Issue as well as, in particular, Adler-Nissen, Galpin, & Rosamond, 2017; Koller, Kopf, & Miglbauer, 2019; Ridge-Newman, Leon-Solis, & O'Donnell, 2018). The article focuses on the discursive logic of various, crisis-driven Brexit imaginaries as expressed across the studied 'prototypical' national contexts and national public spheres in Europe. The main aim is, thereby, to conduct a discourse-conceptual analysis at the intersection of constructions of the 'imagined' and the 'real'. This is done in order to highlight how the discursive conceptualisation of Brexit was not only geared towards constructing an imaginary crisis but also how it was effectively made real by recontextualising various social/political/economic crises thus allowing for the de facto description of Brexit as one of the most significant critical occurrences in post-War Europe. By the same token, the study highlights the predominance of the past/present-to-future dimension of discourse which served as a tool in connecting the 'imaginary' and the 'real' by allowing the discursive linkage of lived collective experiences with various scenarios and projections for the common UK, European or international future.

The starting point for such a cross-national analysis is the assumption that while in the UK itself the 'Brexiteers' and other supporters of Brexit – including, unfortunately, a significant part of the UK media – were strategically downplaying the critical nature of UK's eventual decision to leave the EU (see above), the wider European discourse would see it as predominantly – and rightly – a 'crisis' of varied nature, and as a generally very negative development for both the present and the future of the EU and wider Europe. The article therefore aims to show how wide and diverse the importance of Brexit has been in European news media and how diversified was its meaning as a 'crisis' across the studied European public spheres.

2. Crisis imaginaries, media and cross-national perceptions

2.1. Experienced/expected crises and the ideological nature of the imaginary

Crisis is perhaps one of the most widely debated concepts in social and political sciences which over the course of history has not only been defined by intellectual ideas but also often served as a tool in mobilising social and political action. Reinhart Koselleck, who is among the key modern thinkers to have looked at how the nature and meaning of crisis has evolved historically, points out that crisis – as well as ideas thereof – have almost always been related to the significant moments of social and political transformation when their use significantly increased. Traditionally, the increased use of ideas and imaginaries of crisis have denoted an abrupt and highly transformative moments of vital 'epochal change' (Koselleck, 2006, p. 358) or signalled 'a critical transition period after which – if not everything, then much – will be different' (Koselleck, 2006, p. 358). In late modernity, however, crisis has increasingly come to denote 'a state of greater or lesser permanence, as in a longer or shorter transition towards something better or worse or towards something altogether different' (Koselleck, 2006, p. 358).

Yet while crisis as well as its use as a socially- and politically-mobilising concept/idea has surely been entangled within the said path-dependencies, its discursive construction has traditionally relied on a specific placement at the historical past-to-future axis. Crisis hence often allowed projection of past into the future and vice versa, including as a token of ideologically relating historical/past experience to the thinking about and predicting the future. Crisis has, differently put, been very strongly entangled in the famous Koselleckian dichotomy between 'scope of experience' and 'horizon of expectations' (Koselleck, 1979) which effectively intertwined socially-shared experience of the past with collectively-fuelled ideas and predictions or expectations towards the future. Therein, crisis has often been shown as directly linked to experience of the past 'whose events have been incorporated and can be remembered' (Koselleck, 2004, p. 259) as well as to the projection of the future via 'hope and fear, wishes and desires, cares and rational analysis, receptive display and curiosity' (Koselleck, 2004, p. 259).

The past-to-future thinking about crisis to large extent makes it into a peculiar form an *imaginary* (see, inter alia, Taylor, 2004) that not only serves past/present-related description but also, or perhaps in particular, a powerful ideological future projection (Wolin, 1989). Within such an imaginary, the combination of the 'known' (or the experienced) and the 'unknown' (the expected) still remains central while what is conceived by the imagination is not a mere improvement but a quantum leap that nonetheless preserves elements of the familiar (…) while a strong element of fantasy may figure the imaginary, there is likely to be a significant 'real', verifiable element as well. (Wolin, 2008, p. 18; see also Wolin, 2004)

Accordingly, discourses on crisis have traditionally relied on a combination of the 'real' and the 'projected' while often forming a peculiar form of a socially constructed utopia i.e. 'not just a dream to be enjoyed but a vision to be pursued' (Levitas, 2011, p. 1; see also Graham, 2019). This has opened crisis to a strongly ideological use in particular as part of top-down projections of various formats of social and political action that could/ should result in a change – and hopefully an improvement – of the social reality. Within such discourse, crisis has, however, often effectively ceased to be a description of the 'real' and became to large extent an idea invented for 'political' motives (Sum & Jessop, 2013, p. 396). Yet, driven ideologically, crisis could well also be placed in a reverse discursive trajectory: it could be ignored and disclaimed even if it existed with the thus constructed discourse of disregarding the crisis symptomatic for the populist politics of post-truth and denial.

2.2. Crisis and mediated cross-national perceptions, and the European public sphere

Debating and communicating crises relies very strongly on their discursive construction in the public sphere and, in particular, the media. The latter allows articulating crises by emphasising the role of certain ideas, actions or of (courses of) events as critical. Media thus largely carry the task of constructing crisis/es as events/occurrences that 'disrupt accepted views of the world and how to "go on" within it and also call established theoretical and policy paradigms into question' (Sum & Jessop, 2013, p. 358). Though often doing so out of their own ideological and/or politico-economic interests, media also often undertake a far-reaching critique of not only the ideas of crises – or interpretation of events/actions as such – but also of various scenarios of how they should be 'tackled' or otherwise averted or addressed. They do so while, in particular, building a stance towards politics and the political.

The connection between 'media' and 'crisis' has traditionally been very strong in the context of the mass media (Raboy & Dagenais, 1992; Street, 2011) but probably especially at the politics-media intersection that remains pivotal within, in particular, discourses of the national public spheres. As many classic studies over the years have shown (see, in particular, Hall, Critcher, Jefferson, Clarke, & Roberts, 1978; Schlesinger, 1991), media have played a pivotal part in not only representing but also developing interpretation of national (political, economic, or social) crises. They have also played a crucial role in forging and mediating connections between crises and the wider social phenomena and attitudes as is evident with regard to such central issues as e.g. immigration or social class (see Krzyżanowski, 2009, 2018; Krzyżanowska & Krzyżanowski, 2018; see also Krzyżanowski, Triandafyllidou, & Wodak, 2018).

But crisis-driven discourses have, in particular, been a central feature of the cross-national perception-building by the media as element of 'foreign news' (Hannerz, 2004). Therein, 'foreign' crises have traditionally been among the key triggers for media reporting and media interpretations of foreign events (see, in particular, Galtung & Rugge, 1965). The widely disputed media processes of 'domestication' of foreign news (Gurevitch & Levy, 1990) have also, very prominently, focussed on various types of crises which have not only been discursively represented in the news but were also framed – i.e. interpreted – by means of various nationally-specific i.e. domestic frames (Alasuutari, Qadir, & Creutz, 2013; Clausen, 2004).

In the post-War European context, mediated foreign (national) 'crises' have also been the key triggers of debates that brought contestation of the present and the future of intra-European relations (Triandafyllidou, Wodak, & Krzyżanowski, 2009). However, even some of the significant post-war European events of transnational resonance – such as, e.g. the 1968 student revolt – have not been able to break the strongly domestically-bound tendencies of European news media. The latter, namely, clearly preferred to apply various types of 'national filters' (Krzyżanowski, 2009) in their discursive representations of crises. By doing so, they have often disallowed the development of any wider, cross-national or outright 'European' patterns of interpretation of crises and instead strongly favoured to see reported/mediated events/occurrences through the lens of national interests and ideologies.

The said tendency was not broken even in the more recent media discourses and despite the repeated calls for a more transnational and/or global outlook in the news (Bromley & Slavtcheva-Petkova, 2019; Cottle, 2009) substantiated in the European context by, in particular, the extensive political as well as academic discourse on the 'European Public Sphere' (Koopmans & Statham, 2009; Krzyżanowski, Triandafyllidou, & Wodak, 2009). Therein, many calls have been made to break with the traditional national media tendencies harmful to post-national European thinking and to look for not only representations but also common, transnational patterns of interpretation – including of crises – as profoundly European in nature (Koopmans & Erbe, 2004; Krzyżanowski, 2012).

Yet, while the strictly-national interpretation of foreign/European crises remains the key pattern of interpreting both national and transnational critical occurrences and events, recent years have brought a vital change in the perception and discursive construction of crisis. First, with the arrival of, in particular, the 'economic crisis' as well as its national, European and global variants in the first decade of 2000s, 'crisis' has yet again become one of the central concepts in the wider public European – including media and political – discourse (see e.g. Jessop, 2015; Wodak & Angouri, 2014). Secondly, and even more importantly, crisis has since become a concept that is widely used in political and media discourse to predict *future* trajectories of political and social dynamics often while, paradoxically, being deployed as a description of the changing *current* political, economic or social conditions. Thereby, crisis has become a peculiar tool of discursive *'pre-legitimation'* (Krzyżanowski, 2014) of the present and the future and of, especially, political actions which, while often purely imaginary, are put forward to avert various real and imagined 'crises'. This tendency has, importantly, allowed huge openness and ambivalence as to the definition of what 'crisis' actually is, or what essentially makes one. It enabled 'crisis' to become an element of utopian visions of an *'imaginary reconstitution of society'* (Levitas, 2014) that can easily be re-defined, re-appropriated and claimed/disclaimed by various political and actors, often in a populist and politically-opportunistic fashion (Krzyżanowski, 2018; Wodak & Krzyżanowski, 2017).

3. Brexit and 'crisis' imaginary in European news media: analysis

3.1. Aims and methods of analysis

In its critical discourse analysis of the Brexit and crisis connection in European news media, the present study utilises the methodological pathway of the so-called 'discourse-conceptual analysis' (Krzyżanowski, 2010, 2016; Krzyżanowski & Wodak, 2011). The latter combines key insights from, on the one hand, the Discourse-Historical Approach in Critical Discourse Studies (Krzyżanowski, 2010; Wodak, 2001) and, on the other hand, the so-called conceptual history – or *Begriffsgeschichte* –of Reinhart Koselleck (1979, 2002, 2004 and above) and his followers.

Drawing on such a methodological combination, the analysis presented below aims to examine how the social and political concept of 'Brexit' is constructed in the analysed media discourses on the back of reporting about the results and implications of UK 2016 Referendum on Leaving the EU. The analysis is event-specific and comparative i.e. it looks at various nationally-specific discourses about the UK Brexit referendum as well as points to similarities and/or differences between the studied nationally-specific discursive representations and interpretations of Brexit in the context of mediated reporting.

Specifically, the conducted critical discourse analysis is argumentation-oriented (Krzyżanowski, 2010) i.e. it is deployed in order to discover the key arguments that are used to frame the discursive Brexit-crisis connection in the analysed media. Therein, the central aim is to explore in-depth the key argumentative frames – or *topoi* – that summarise arguments which are constructed for/against the key debated ideas and views.

Further to a close look into *argumentation* including deployment of context-specific (i.e. content-driven) as well as classic (i.e. structure-driven) topoi and fallacies (Krzyżanowski, 2010; Reisigl & Wodak, 2001), other/investigated discursive strategies included (a) *representation of social actors along with construction (or denial) of their agency* or their pivotal role (or lack thereof) in undertaking/driving or undergoing the described social and political action (Reisigl & Wodak, 2001; van Leeuwen, 2008) and (b) *presupposition* i.e. 'taken-for granted, implicit claim embedded within the explicit meaning of a text' (Richardson, 2007, p. 63). These strategies were often used within a further strategy of (c) *pre-legitimation of practice* (Krzyżanowski, 2014) which showed future/projected events as prototypically(possibly) following the known and established course of events and thus being legitimised by way of 'usual' patterns and path-dependencies of social and political action (van Leeuwen, 2007).

While the in-depth look at these and other discursive strategies has allowed discovering the key in-depth features of the analysed media discourses and arguments, at a more abstract level the analysis has also aimed at establishing the aforementioned discourse-conceptual connection. The latter is be displayed by, inter alia, the overall 'semantic field' of the 'Brexit' concept (see Figure 2) that provides a generalised representation of the key crisis-related ideas attached to the central concept. This also serves as a map of key argumentative lines (*topoi*) through which the 'Brexit' concept was constructed (i.e. argued for/against) and thereby particularised in/via crisis-oriented discourse along both nationally-specific or ideological (liberal vs. conservative) lines.

3.2. Research design and empirical material

The study covers media representations in four European countries which are viewed as prototypical for various ideas/visions of European politics and carrying different types and length of experience of EU membership:

(a) *Austria* – a central-European country which became EU member in 1995 and is also one of the members of the Eurozone. While Austria has traditionally had high levels of support for European integration and has also been crucial in EU-coordinated actions (e.g, such as those with regard to the recent 2015–16 European 'refugee crisis'), the growing insurgence of right-wing populist politics in the country since early 2000s has spread a number of Eurosceptic ideas and tendencies that increasingly penetrate into the country's mainstream politics and mainstream media. The latter remain, however, largely pro-European with liberal Austrian newspapers in favour of EU and the conservative ones remaining of moderate yet still pro-European stance.

(b) *Germany* – one of the Western-European founding states of the European integration project and its key driving force since the 1950s. Germany has traditionally had high levels of support for EU across the political spectrum and in both liberal and conservative media. While the long-term rule of the Christian-Democratic German Chancellor Angela Merkel (in office since 2005) assures continuity of the country's strongly pro-European politics – and its de-facto and symbolic leadership of the EU bloc and the Eurozone – the growing criticism of the chancellor (e.g. in the Conservative media) often brings more 'realistic' (i.e. moderately-critical) approach to European politics often tied to personalisation of EU failures – such as e.g. Brexit – as Merkel's own political mistakes.

(c) *Poland* – a central/eastern European country which was the leader of the 'big bang' 2004 EU enlargement. Poland has traditionally had strong pro-European views which have been further sustained by the country's significant economic and infrastructural development since becoming EU member . Polish pro-European stance has, however, been very strongly contested with the arrival of new right-wing populist parties – most notably Law and Justice or PiS – that have been in power since 2015 and often aimed to align Polish politics with that of such Eurosceptic and EU-defiant CEE states as e.g. Hungary. Despite that, in recent years Poland's liberal (commercial) media have remained very strongly pro-European while right-wing as well as state-controlled public media have at the same time become increasingly Eurosceptic often acquiring radical features and/or openly questioning Poland's EU membership or the plausibility of the EU project as such.

(d) *Sweden* – a northern-European state which, just like Austria, joined the EU in 1995 yet, similarly to other Scandinavian EU members (e.g. Denmark) decided to remain outside the Eurozone. Sweden has traditionally good levels of support for the EU in line with its pro-European social-democratic as well as moderate-conservative politics. However, Sweden perceives its EU membership as far more pragmatic and less organic than e.g. that of such countries as Germany or France, as is also symbolised by its decision not to adopt the Euro. Sweden's mainstream media – esp. broadsheets – are traditionally pro-European though with a clearly critical stance sometimes presented in the

conservative press and a growing criticism of the EU increasingly originating in country's online media and uncivil society or right-wing populist politics.

Within the four studied countries, the article looks at quality and quality-like newspapers in order to capture a spectrum of opinion-making voices within the studied national contexts as well as sample a variety of Europe-related views. In most cases, the ideological polaris-ation of views is moderate and oscillates between a liberal and openly pro-European newspaper and a conservative or moderately pro-European – or 'Euro-realistic' – one. This logic is, however, different in one case – of Poland – where the polarisation between a strongly pro-European liberal newspaper and an overtly Eurosceptic radical-conservative counterpart is evident.

The material for the analysis was collected from databases run by the newspapers them-selves (in Poland) or from nationally-specific press archives (*Wiso-Presse* for Austria and Germany, and *Mediearkivet* for Sweden). The analysis was limited to press texts with images generally not included. The analysed material was collected by way of a database keyword search focussing on 'Brexit' (or 'brexit') and excluding much wider and highly poly-semous keywords like the 'UK' or 'United Kingdom' (and their equivalents in German, Polish or Swedish). The material was collected and analysed in the original languages i.e. German, Polish and Swedish. The material was not collected in a genre specific way and hence it included both news-reporting and opinion/editorial genres. However, as a result of the keyword-driven search a clear preference for the opinion-making commentaries/editorials and related genres could be observed across all studied countries and newspapers.

The empirical material was collected within the scope of, altogether, 4 months (ca. 16 weeks) i.e. between 1 May and 31 August 2016. The aim was for the empirical material to encompass ca. 8 weeks before and 8 weeks after the UK Brexit referendum of 23 June 2016 in order to observe the key tendencies along the growing or falling frequency/volume of reporting which, expectedly, was the most sizeable in late June and early July 2016 i.e. in the immediate aftermath of the UK referendum. While the empirical material created a corpus of 3720 articles, the eventual in-depth, qualitative analysis presented below was undertaken on a much smaller sample of ca. 200 articles published on the day of the UK Brexit referendum (23 June 2016) and in the immediately following 6 days (thus forming the so-called sample reporting week; depending on the existence of weekend/ Sunday editions etc.).

As Figure 1 indicates, in all analysed countries except Poland there was (a) a generally very large interest in the UK Brexit referendum and (b) in all studied countries the conser-vative press reported UK referendum more extensively than its liberal counterparts. Inter-estingly, the most sizeable nationally-specific corpus was that of Austria (1346 articles altogether) with the conservative *Die Presse* (PR) yielding 703 articles and liberal *Der Stan-dard* (ST) publishing 643 pieces. The German corpus was the second largest and yielded 1160 articles with conservative/nationwide *Die Welt* (WE, 664 articles) outnumbering its liberal counterpart i.e Berlin-based *Tagesspiegel* (TS, 496 articles). The Swedish corpus came third with 1016 articles and a similar discrepancy between the conservative *Svenska Dagbladet* (SvD, 443 articles) and the liberal *Dagens Nyheter* (DN, 352 articles). Finally, the Polish corpus clearly stood out from all other corpora having yielded only 198 articles altogether (i.e. only ca. 15% of the German or 20% of the Austrian corpus). In the Polish corpus, liberal and pro-European *Gazeta Wyborcza* (GW, 135 articles)

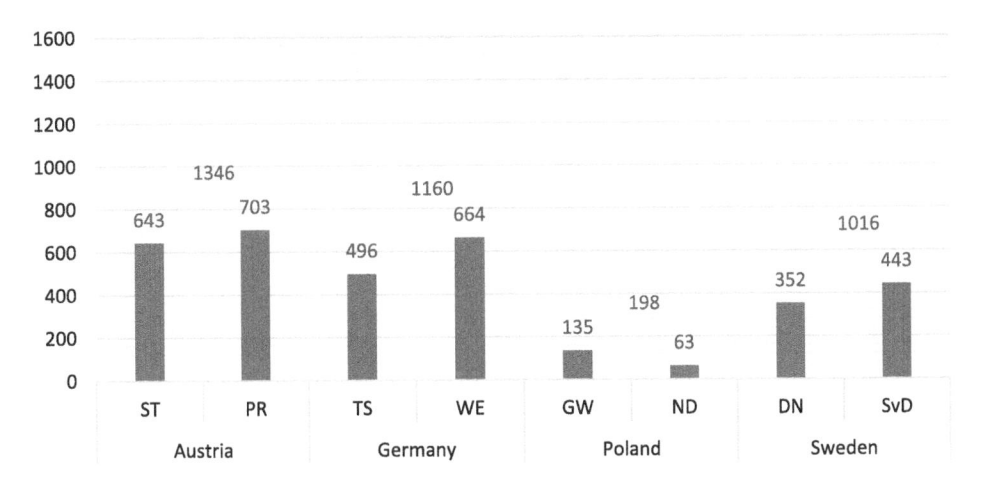

Figure 1. Analysed newspaper corpora per newspaper/country.

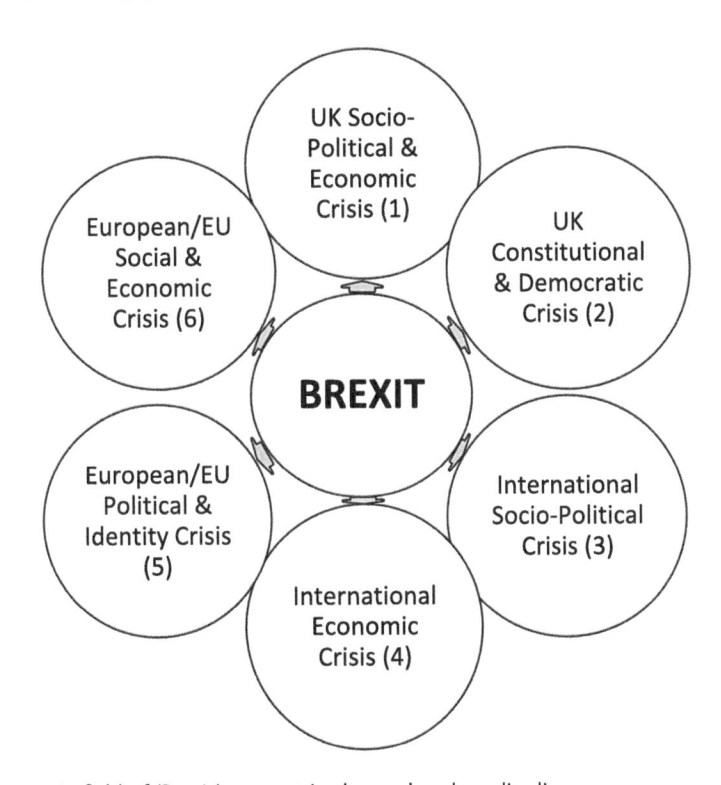

Figure 2. Semantic field of 'Brexit' concept in the analysed media discourse.

catered for almost 70% of all articles with the radical-conservative and Eurosceptic *Nasz Dziennik* (ND) yielding altogether only 63 articles.

3.3. Overview of key topoi at the Brexit/crisis intersection

Figure 2, which summarises the core arguments in all of the analysed countries, presents the semantic field of the 'Brexit' concept along with the key crisis-related *topoi* that were deployed in the analysed media reporting (see below for examples). As the figure suggests, 'Brexit' was extensively related to crisis in a discourse which run along three main dimensions that were, respectively, UK-, internationally- and Europe/EU-specific. Each of those dimensions further comprised two topoi including looking at Brexit as: *UK Socio-Political and Economic Crisis* (Topos 1), *UK Constitutional and Democratic Crisis* (Topos 2), *International Socio-Political Crisis* (Topos 3), *International Economic Crisis* (Topos 4) and *European/EU Political and Identity Crisis* (Topos 5) or *European/EU Social & Economic Crisis* (Topos 6).

The first topos – of *Brexit as UK Socio-Political and Economic Crisis* – was probably the widest of all deployed in the analysed discourse. It argued that Brexit is, first and foremost, a result of ongoing divisions and malaise in the UK society and economy and that it will further solidify the ongoing crisis in UK's 'broken' and divided society. The discursive constructions of this topos often entailed various 'on the ground' looks at the current/future implications of Brexit – including via 'vox-pops' and other quotes from the general UK public (often in a form of so-called straw-man fallacies) – and boiled down to social actor representation of the British public by via e.g. classification of social actors as different kinds of 'people'. Some aspects of argumentation embedded within this topos were also about the deceitful nature of the 'Leave' campaign in the UK which could eventually lead to a crisis of UK public life as well as the eventual future 'Bregret' of the British public (see nationally-specific findings in 2.2, below, for examples).

Often connected to the latter, the second topos of *Brexit as a UK Constitutional & Democratic Crisis* focussed specifically on long-term UK-internal democratic implications of the referendum. Realisations of this topos often departed from presupposition of UK as profoundly divided country – as evidenced through, in particular, the varied nationally-specific outcomes of the Brexit vote in England, Scotland, Wales and Northern Ireland. Through these, it was also often presupposed that the UK is an artificial state construct. Here, references to, in particular, Scotland were central including arguments that, since it overwhelmingly voted to remain in the EU, Scotland might acquire the right to yet another independence referendum now that the rest of the UK has decided to leave the EU. However, the main gist of the second topos remained future oriented: it was encompassed by the argument that Brexit would, effectively, contribute to the crisis of UK as a 'Union' as well as profoundly undermine the current format of British state system as a constitutional/parliamentary monarchy. Brexit, hence, would eventually be the foundation of, it was often predicted, the future end of UK's 'union' in the current form.

Opening the international dimension of the analysed transnational discourse, the third topos – of *Brexit as an International Socio-Political Crisis* – drew on the premise that Brexit is not only a foundation of UK-specific or European current/future crisis but that its future implications would be strongly international if not outright global in nature. Often drawing on extensive presuppositions, this topos was the main vehicle of the 'domestication' of Brexit in/into the various analysed national contexts. There, it was often implied that various societies internationally, as well as their constituent social groups and social actors (e.g. Polish workers as migrants, including in the UK), will be profoundly affected by the Brexit process. Brexit hence was seen as thus contributing to international socio-political crisis which may not only be limited to the explicitly-related national contexts (e.g. Poland and the UK, Sweden and the UK etc.) but may have cross-national implications and result in, inter alia, solidification of not only social malaise but also of related types ofpolitical change (e.g. further rise of xenophobia or right-wing populist tendencies, etc).

The fourth topos of *Brexit as International Economic Crisis* followed the usual pattern of debating global economic implications of a political crisis. Brexit vote was hence seen as having profound implications for the future shape of European as well as wider world economy while many scenarios of economic uncertainty and recession also being provided. This strongly future-oriented topos was driven by a peculiar uncertainty about economic implications of Brexit in view of the fact that, as such, it has no actual precedence and hence many key economic actors – in UK, Europe and beyond –remained uncertain about the possibility of future economic ties to the UK or of the impact of Brexit on the wider stability of Europe's cross-national economic ties. The topos also operated along a peculiar macro-micro logic: while macro-level global implications were often considered across the studied material so was also the impact of Brexit on small and mid-size enterprises whose ability to work and collaborate cross-nationally is strongly dependent on the EU frameworks.

The topos of *Brexit as European/EU Political and Identity Crisis* – listed as fifth above and probably the most frequent in the analysed corpus – opened up the EU/Europe-specific dimension of the analysed cross-national media discourse. This topos showed Brexit as a symptom of an ongoing crisis of the European integration project and, while allowing for the fact that the UK has traditionally been an 'awkward partner' in the EU and its predecessors, it saw Brexit as having profound impact on the future of the EU now put into question and thrown into further crisis. This topos included traditional aspects of internationally-oriented media discourse like, e.g. the overview of different countries and political actor's 'reactions' to the Brexit vote often tied with predictions about EU and Europe's future. It also presented social, political as well as economic sources of the current EU/European crisis among which the upsurge of Eurosceptic right-wing populism was almost always put to the foreground. Since, in line with the topos, it was argued that right-wing populist politics – along with its ongoing attempts to, allegedly, 'reform' but effectively undermine the EU – would, it was expected, prevail in Europe in the foreseeable future, it should also be expected that the crisis of the EU symptomatized and emphasised by Brexit was set to continue well into the future.

Finally, the sixth topos – of *Brexit as European/EU Social and Economic Crisis* – allowed media writers to skilfully connect the national and the cross-national plains to argue that, while a political move in itself, Brexit would have a profound impact on the wider European society and economy. The topos relied on various strategies – of e.g. collectivised or individualised representation of social actors etc. – aimed to portray wider sections of society and social groups as currently and potentially affected by Brexit and UK's leaving the EU. The topos was also one that nested the various references to intra-European migration while pointing that various migrant groups (e.g. various EU citizens in the UK) will bear the brunt of Brexit decisions 'on the ground'. Brexit, it was predicted by means of the topos, could also lead to a wider European 'social' crisis as well as a far-reaching change of mood in social and intergroup relations and attitudes towards, in particular, immigration.

3.4. Country-specific deployment of key topoi at the Brexit/crisis intersection

3.4.1. Austria

The peculiarity of the analysed Austrian liberal media discourse was that, contrary to the other studied outlets/countries, it very strongly focussed on the UK-internal dimensions and ontologies of Brexit as a crisis. The main line of argumentation in the Austrian *Der Standard* (ST) was therefore one aligned with Topos 2 which focussed on the UK Constitutional and Democratic Crisis. This topos allowed the authors to not only claim that, as such, the UK constitutional system was heavily strained and flawed, but that Brexit as such was symptomatic for a rather certain, forthcoming 'falling into pieces' of the EU (see Example 1). As the example also emphasises, the Brexit thinking in the UK was driven by mainly flawed and wrong ideas which might have lead to the fact that as a result of the Brexit process the UK would eventually end up in a much less favourable political/economic position than as an EU member. It is also mentioned metaphorically that the 'most bitter irony of history' ('*die bitterste Ironie der Geschichte*)' would be a situation whereby the Brexit process would contribute to the fall of the UK with, inter alia, Scottish independence or reunification of Ireland.

> EXAMPLE 1:
>
> *Das Vereinigte Königreich wird möglicherweise zerfallen. Was übrig bleibt, wäre Kleinbritannien, bestehend aus England und Wales. Das Brexit-Lager wollte Großbritannien wieder unabhängig machen. Das wird sich als Illusion herausstellen, wenn am Schluss der Austrittsverhandlungen ein assoziierter Status herauskommt, bei dem die Briten die Regeln der EU übernehmen müssen, ohne sie mitgestalten zu können. Aber die bitterste Ironie der Geschichte wäre es, wenn die britischen Nationalisten zu Geburtshelfern der Unabhängigkeit Schottlands und der Wiedervereinigung Irlands würden.* ST 25/06/2016, p. 43
>
> The United Kingdom could well fall into pieces. What could be left is a 'Small Britain' consisting of England and Wales. The Brexit camp wanted to make Great Britain sovereign again. This will prove to be an illusion if the exit negotiations end up in an associated status in which the British have to accept the EU rules without the possibility of creating them. But the most bitter irony of history would be such if the British nationalists assisted the birth of the independence of Scotland or of the reunification of Ireland.

The strongly UK-internal focus in the studied Austrian liberal press was also displayed in the use of Topos 1 (UK Socio-Political and Economic Crisis) which allowed overtly describing Brexit as a potential 'disaster' ('*Desaster*', see Example 2) whose roots were mainly economic and politico–economic in nature. Brexit, it was argued, would be a direct reason for UK entering into (yet another) recession with obvious economic and wider social implications.

> EXAMPLE 2:
>
> *Für Großbritannien wird der Austritt ein ökonomisches Desaster. Die Verlagerung von Produktionsstandorten und die Einbußen im internationalen Handel werden das Königreich laut Experten in eine tiefe Rezession stürzen.* ST 25/06/2016, p. 44
>
> The exit will be an economic disaster for Great Britain. According to the experts, the moving of manufacturing sites and the losses in international trade will throw the UK into a deep recession.

Finally, in addition to the UK-internal foci, the Austrian liberal discourse also focussed on the EU/Europe dimension by specifically addressing Brexit in the context of the European/

EU Political and Identity Crisis (Topos 5). Unlike in many instances of the conservative media discourses, the focus here was not, however, on the mistakes/flaws of the EU but on the pan-European pandemic of right-wing populism and Euroscepticism – very poignantly nominated/predicated as 'pan-European nationalistic revisionism' ('*gesamteuropäische nationalistische Revisionismus*', see Example 3) – that holds the main responsibility for creating a crisis of the European integration project symptomized by Brexit. The ontology of that crisis was pointed to explicitly within a combination of, on the one hand, the (tabloid) media power, and, on the other, the revival of the still unbroken historical nationalism across the EU. All of these were coined/nominated as a peculiar ideological 'mixture' ('*Mixtur*') that fuelled Brexit and undermined the EU while repeatedly putting forward the image of 'Europe as the enemy' ('*Feindbild Europa*').

EXAMPLE 3:

Der Ausgang des Referendums bedroht die Integration Europas. Das Votum des britischen Wahlvolks stärkt die radikale Rechte und die Nationalismen in nahezu allen Mitgliedsstaaten. Der gesamteuropäische nationalistische Revisionismus hat sich bereits in Position gebracht. Eine brisante, vom Boulevard geschürte Mixtur aus ungebrochenen nationalistischen Mentalitäten, Provinzialismen und Globalisierungsängsten hat den Rechtspopulismus hier wie dort, Hofer und Brexit, groß und salonfähig gemacht. Seine Identität bezieht er, übrigens ganz logisch, aus dem Feindbild Europa. ST 25/06/2016, p. 43

The outcome of the referendum endangers the European integration. The vote of the British electorate strengthens the radical right and nationalisms in almost every [EU] member state. The pan-European nationalistic revisionism is now well in place. It is fuelled by the boulevard [press], by explosive mixture of continued nationalistic mentalities, by provincialisms and by fears of globalisation all making right wing-populism here and there, Hofer and Brexit, big and socially acceptable. Its identity rests, in fact quite logically, on the image of Europe as the enemy.

While the Austrian liberal press focused explicitly on various ontologies of Brexit as a national/European crisis, its conservative counterparts mainly constructed their discourse around future crisis scenarios epitomised by the Brexit vote. Here, the focus of the Austrian *Die Presse* (PR) revolved mainly around the economic crisis (to be) ignited by the Brexit vote as encompassed by, in particular, Topos 4 on International Economic Crisis. What is emphasised in Example 4, is the fact that the international markets were negatively surprised, or 'caught cold' ('*kalt erwischt*'), with, inter alia, the banking sector largely unprepared for the market lows caused by the Brexit vote. The general danger pointed to was that of the 'insecurity' ('*Unsicherheit*') or lack of clarity which, known to be decisive for market volatility etc., symbolised the vision of the crisis period that will come in the aftermath, and as a result of, the UK referendum. In a similar vein jobs that would 'depart' ('*abwandern*') from the UK were constructed as a symbol of 'crisis' and 'loss' that would be a result of Brexit.

EXAMPLE 4:

Der Brexit hat die Märkte am Freitag wirklich kalt erwischt. Nach den Umfragen der vergangenen Woche war die Angst vor einem Austritts-Votum am Donnerstag verpufft. Es folgte, wovor der Währungsspekulant George Soros gewarnt hatte: ein schwarzer Freitag an den Börsen. Am schlimmsten hat es die Banken erwischt. Was in diesem Sektor geschehen wird, ist nach dem Brexit-Votum völlig unklar. In der City of London arbeiten rund 700.000 Menschen im Finanzsektor. Ein Teil dieser Jobs wird wohl abwandern - etwa nach Dublin oder Frankfurt. Die Unsicherheit machte sich am Freitag auch in den Aktienkursen bemerkbar. PR 25/06/2016, pp. 10–11.

Brexit caught the markets cold on Friday. Polls last week still maintained that the fear of the [UK] exit vote on Thursday largely evaporated. But what followed was, just as the currency trader George Soros warned, a black Friday on the stock exchanges. What will happen in the sector after the Brexit vote remains unclear. Around 700.000 people work in the financial sector in the City of London. A large part of those jobs could well depart – possibly for Dublin or Frankfurt. The uncertainty could also be noted in the stock indices on Friday.

Another set of future predictions of crisis in the Austrian conservative press were framed by Topos 5 (EU Political/Identity Crisis) where the main tone of the reporting was characterised by a peculiar 'Schadenfreude' i.e. the fact that Brexit was to large extent an expectable symptom of some long-standing, and long unaddressed, EU-political and -institutional mistakes and errors. Brexit was thereby shown as just one in a series of EU crises – 'for years one crisis haunts the next in the EU' (*'Seit Jahren jagt in der Union eine Krise die nächste'*) – which, however, may eventually lead to a 'dissolution' (*'Auflösung'*) or to 'the fall of the EU' (*'EU-Zerfall'*) and to the subsequent 'exits' by further EU member states. Here, however, the past-to-future connection was established by foregrounding the aforementioned rise of right-wing populism and nationalism as well as by arguing that the European citizenry has long lost touch with the European project while civic 'trust' (*'Vertrauen'*) in the EU project has also gradually evaporated (see Example 5).

EXAMPLE 5:

Seit Jahren jagt in der Union eine Krise die nächste - und selbst für die größten Optimisten fällt auch eine Auflösung der europäischen Staatengemeinschaft längst nicht mehr in den Bereich des Unmöglichen. Austrittstendenzen gibt es in mehreren Mitgliedstaaten, EU-kritische Parteien sind europaweit im Aufwind. Der Grund: Vielerorts haben die Bürger das Vertrauen in den Mehrwert einer EU-Mitgliedschaft verloren. (…). Die Stimmung im eigenen Land ist für viele Staats- und Regierungschefs der wichtigste Gradmesser, an dem sie ihr Tun und Handeln ausrichten. Kein Wunder also, dass europäische Entscheidungsträger seit Langem darauf hinweisen, dass die Gefahr eines EU-Zerfalls real sei. PR 24/06/2016, p. 1

For years one crisis haunts the next in the EU, and even the biggest optimists have long not thought of the dissolution of the European community as utterly impossible. Tendencies to leave are now present in several member states while the EU-critical political parties are on the rise. The reason: in many places the citizens have lost their trust in the added value of the EU community. (…). The mood in one's own country is for many heads of state and government still the key indicator for how to act. It is not surprising therefore that European decision-makers have long been pointing to the fact that the fall of the EU is realistic.

3.4.2. Germany

The liberal discourse of the German *Tagesspiegel* (TS) largely continued the argumentation encompassed by the aforementioned EU-oriented Topos 5. As Example 6 shows, the said topos allows to call Brexit very explicitly a crisis and even as the EU's 'biggest crisis of its history' (*'die schwerste Krise ihrer Geschichte'*).

EXAMPLE 6:

Großbritannien hat die Europäische Union mit seiner Entscheidung zum Austritt aus der Gemeinschaft in die schwerste Krise ihrer Geschichte gestürzt. Bei dem Volksentscheid am Donnerstag sprachen sich 51,9 Prozent für einen Brexit aus. TS 25/06/2016, p. 1

> Great Britain has put the European Union in the biggest crisis of its history. In the referendum on Thursday, 51.9 percent voted in favour of a Brexit.

Indeed, the same line of arguing was continued even further when, as shown in Example 7, Brexit was called a 'crisis of all crises' ('*Die Krise aller Krisen*') with the crisis-related metaphors not only epitomised by mentioning of a 'Brexit-Schock' but also continued explicitly in the discourse via e.g. predicating EU gathering as a 'European crisis-meeting' ('*ein europäisches Krisentreffen*') or via the recontextualisation of militarising metaphors of agreeing same 'common line' ('*eine gemeinsame Linie*') etc.

EXAMPLE 7:

Die Krise aller Krisen (…) Nach dem Brexit-Schock haben zunächst einmal Politiker der europäischen Gründerstaaten das Wort. (…) Nach dem Treffen der Außenminister steht am Montag in Berlin ein europäisches Krisentreffen in Berlin mit Kanzlerin Angela Merkel (CDU), EU-Ratschef Donald Tusk, Italiens Regierungschef Matteo Renzi und Frankreichs Präsident François Hollande auf dem Programm. Bei der Begegnung wollen die EU-Spitzen eine gemeinsame Linie für den Gipfel der 28 Staats- und Regierungschefs festzurren, der am Dienstag in Brüssel beginnt. Auch der EU-Gipfel wird ganz im Zeichen des Brexit stehen. TS 25/06/2016, p. 4

The crisis of all crises (…) After the Brexit-shock, politicians of the European founding states take the stand (…). After the meeting of foreign ministers now comes the European crisis meeting in Berlin with Chancellor Angela Merkel (CDU), EU Council President Donald Tusk, Italian Prime Minster Matteo Renzi and the French President François Hollande. At the meeting, the EU leaders will set the common line for the summit of 28 heads of state and government beginning next Thursday in Brussels. Brexit will be the key issue at the EU summit.

But, unlike in the e.g. the Austrian discourse which was relatively 'fixed' within specific argument topoi, the German liberal discourse also introduced a combination of arguments as in Example 8 where the central EU-Topos 5 (above) was combined with Topos 3 (International Socio-Political Crisis) enabling a more 'ontological' thinking about the roots of crisis embodied by Brexit. Here, the 'international' crisis was that of rising right-wing populism and nationalism (previously mainly treated as a European problem, see above) seen as a source of crises by, in particular, promoting anew the nationalist and isolationist tendencies. Interestingly, that argument also allowed for the domestication of the argumentation by means of a strategy or perspectivation while e.g. using a quote from the deputy leader of the right-wing populist German AfD who openly criticised Angela Merkel – seen both nationally and internationally as a symbolic leader of the EU – for 'her open borders' in the course of the Refugee Crisis which, as such, have 'driven the British out of the European Union' ('*die Briten aus der Europäischen Union vertrieben*').

EXAMPLE 8:

Die AfD macht zudem Bundeskanzlerin Angela Merkel (CDU) und ihre Flüchtlingspolitik für den EU-Austritt Großbritanniens verantwortlich. "Ich glaube, Frau Merkel hat mit ihren offenen Grenzen die Briten aus der Europäischen Union vertrieben", sagte Parteivize Alexander Gauland am Freitag in Berlin. TS, 25/06/2016, p. 5

The AfD is making the Federal Chancellor Angela Merkel (CDU) and her refugee policy responsible for Great Britain's leaving of the EU. "I believe that with her open borders Ms Merkel has driven the British out of the European Union" said deputy [AfD] leader Alexander Gauland on Friday in Berlin.

But such a combination of arguments – e.g. encompassed by UK-internal Topoi 1 (UK socio-economic crisis) and 2 (UK constitutional/democratic crisis) as in Example 9 – was also used outside of the domesticating tendencies whenever the German liberal media discourse wanted to portray the UK context as a divided kingdom' (*'das gespaltene Königreich'*) both prior to and as a result of the vote on Brexit. The UK was here constructed as driven by an array of long-standing social dichotomies incl. 'the poor against the rich' (*'Arm gegen Reich'*), 'the young against the old' (*'Jung gegen Alt'*), or of 'cities versus countryside' (*'Stadt versus Land'*) which are set to deepen even further as a result of the Brexit vote.

EXAMPLE 9:

Das gespaltene Königreich - Arm gegen Reich, Jung gegen Alt, Stadt versus Land: Nach dem Refer-endum droht Großbritannien entlang demografischer Linien zu zerbrechen. Nirgendwo wird das zurzeit deutlicher als in der Hauptstadt. TS 27/06/2016, p. 3

The divided kingdom – the poor against the rich, the young against the old, and cities versus countryside: after the referendum there Great Britain is in danger of breaking along demographic lines. Nowhere is it as evident right now as in the [UK] capital.

The argumentative compounds/combinations mentioned above were also specific for the conservative discourse of the German *Die Welt* (WE) which, however, combined different sets of arguments embodied by, in particular, Topoi 4 (International Economic Crisis) and 6 (European social and economic crisis). Here (see Example 10), the discourse was dominated by future scenarios of various dimensions of forthcoming economic recession/crisis including 'Recession in Great Britain, Chaos in the EU, billions lost in Germany too' (*'Rezession in Großbritannien, Chaos in der EU, Milliardenverluste auch für Deutschland-'*). But, on the other hand, the issue of 'costs' and, specifically, of defining the economic burden of the UK Brexit decision on remaining European states and their citizens was put to the fore. Strategies of analogy abode in this context when, e.g. the actual costs of Brexit – widely seen as economic crisis – were explicitly set/calculated at 13k Euro per each EU citizen with the metaphorical analogy made to a cost of 'a Volkswagen Polo, 60 hp, Basic trim' (*'ein VW-Polo, 60 PS, Basis-Variante'*).

EXAMPLE 10:

Kurzfristig würde ein Brexit zu heftigen Turbulenzen an den Finanzmärkten führen. Die Börsen würden einbrechen, Pfund und Euro abwerten. Schon in den ersten Stunden könnten Billionen vernichtet werden. Später würde es noch verheerender: Rezession in Großbritannien, Chaos in der EU, Milliarden-verluste auch für Deutschland. Der Brexit würde das gesamte ökonomische Gefüge Europas durchei-nanderbringen. Das Wachstum des Kontinents würde auf Jahre hinaus gemindert. Bricht man all das herunter, rechnet Europas Wohlstandsverluste nach einem Brexit auf die Bürger um, stehen am Ende fast 13.000 Euro. Oder ein VW-Polo, 60 PS, Basis-Variante. WE 23/06/2016, p. 13

In a short run Brexit will lead to heavy turbulences in the financial markets. Stock markets will fall, and the Pound and Euro lose value. Even in the very first hours, millions could be lost. But it would be even more devastating later: recession in Great Britain, chaos in the EU, billions lost in Germany too. Brexit would bring the entire European architecture into disarray. Any growth at the continent would be curbed for years. All this considered, the loss of wealth in Europe would come to almost 13000 Euro per citizen. Or a VW-Polo, 60 hp, Basic trim.

The argumentative compounds mentioned above also served a somewhat different aim of domesticating the Brexit-related crisis developments by showing them as rooted in the actions of German politicians. Here, Angela Merkel was often discursively foregrounded when, somewhat unexpectedly for a German conservative press, she was criticised as standing at the roots of the wider European crisis embodied by the UK Brexit referendum result. Via combination of Topoi 5 (European/EU Political and Identity Crisis) and 3 (International Socio-Political Crisis) it was hence shown that Merkel's and Germany's immigration policy considered in the context of the recent European 'refugee crisis' – all contributed to the 'European disaster in Great Britain' ('*Das europäische Desaster in Großbritannien*'). As Example 11 shows, Merkel was thus also criticised for intervening in domestic issues of other European countries – specifically Greece – while unnecessarily making these into 'Berlin's key issue' ('*Berliner Chefsache*').

EXAMPLE 11

Das europäische Desaster in Großbritannien, das bei allem bitteren Beigeschmack eben auch einen Feiertag der Volkssouveränität bedeutet, rückt jetzt die eigentliche, von Medien und Eliten hochgelobte Frau ins Zentrum, die vielen bereits als inoffizielle Kanzlerin von Europa galt. Angela Merkel machte die Euro-Krise in Griechenland im Doppelpass mit ihrem Finanzminister zur Berliner Chefsache. WE, 25/06/2016, p. 1.

The European disaster in Great Britain, which even with all the bitter taste means a celebration of popular sovereignty, now puts into the spotlight a woman praised by media and elites and many other as Europe's Chancellor. Together with her finance ministers, Angel Merkel made the Euro-crisis in Greece into Berlin's key issue.

3.4.3. Poland

Though least sizeable of all, the liberal discourse of the Polish daily *Gazeta Wyborcza* (GW) probably remained the richest in terms of the array of arguments and topoi used to frame its reporting and interpretations of the Brexit referendum. While the majority of the individual and compounded arguments here were strongly domesticated in the Polish discourse – as in Example 12 – they relatively unanimously showed that Brexit was set to become a crisis in all areas of life ranging from everyday, social and family life (Topos 3; e.g. via growing interest rates or mortgage costs) to wider international economy (Topos 4) and international as well as European geopolitics (Topos 5). There, it was argued, Brexit would be a metaphorical 'shock' to the Union, Poland and the entire world' ('*byłby wstrząsem dla Unii, Polski i całego świata*').

EXAMPLE 12:

Dla Polaków wyższe raty kredytów we frankach i euro oraz droższe tegoroczne wakacje. W przyszłości: zamknięcie dla nas brytyjskiego rynku pracy. Brexit byłby wstrząsem dla Unii, Polski i całego świata, dotknąłby każdej sfery naszego życia. GW 27/06/2016, p. 6.

Higher interest rate for Swiss-Franc credits and more expensive holidays for the Poles. In the future: closure of the British job market for us. Brexit would be a shock to the Union, Poland and the entire world, and it would affect each possible sphere of our lives.

In both the example above and in the majority of the GW liberal corpus, Polish migrants in the UK were often highlighted/foregrounded – though not always activated – as a group that symbolises the eventual repercussions of Brexit. Within realisation of Topos 6 (European/EU Social and Economic Crisis) related to the European identity topos 4, Polish migrants in the UK were seen as a group of those bearing 'on the ground' the brunt of UK nationalism and anti-immigration ideology embodied by the Brexit decisions. Within this chain of argumentation, individual life stories and narratives of (non) belonging by Polish migrants 'caught' in the Brexit predicament were often quoted. In Example 13, using a *pars pro toto* argumentation, a Polish resident in the UK was quoted saying that 'by voting to leave the EU, the British voted against me' (*'Brytyjczycy, głosując za opuszczeniem UE, zagłosowali przeciwko mnie'*).

EXAMPLE 13:

Po raz pierwszy, odkąd jestem w Anglii, czuję się tu niechciana. Brytyjczycy, głosując za opuszcze- niem UE, zagłosowali przeciwko mnie - mówi Maria. Ma 27 lat. Studiowała na Wyspach, a od trzech lat mieszka i pracuje w Bristolu. GW 25/06/2016 p. 8

It is for the first time since I have been in England that I feel so unwanted here. By voting to leave the EU, the British voted against me – says Maria. She is 27. She studied in the UK and has now been living and working in Bristol for three years.

But Polish liberal GW also provided wider, macro-political lines of thinking (see Example 14), in particular by constructing Brexit as thehistorically most significant crisis of recent years. Remaining with the Topos 5 (European EU/Identity Crisis), the discourse allowed the Polish liberal daily to construct it – by means of multiple predicates enclosed in extended nominal clause – as 'an event carrying the most repercussions since the Fall of the Berlin Wall' (*'wydarzeniem najbardziej brzemiennym w skutki od zburzenia muru ber- lińskiego'*) which would also bring long-term negative implications to European politics, especially by the further rise of right-wing populism and anti-immigration attitudes (including, notably, against the Polish migrants).

EXAMPLE 14:

Brexit będzie dla Europy wydarzeniem najbardziej brzemiennym w skutki od zburzenia muru ber- lińskiego. Oczywiście, kierunek trudnych do precyzyjnego prognozowania wydarzeń byłby prze- ciwny do pełnych proeuropejskiego entuzjazmu decyzji po upadku żelaznej kurtyny. Wygrana Brexitu dodałaby siły eurosceptykom i przeciwnikom UE w innych krajach Unii, m.in. Holandii. Możliwe, że szantażując referendami o wyjściu z UE, zaczęliby jeszcze głośniej żądać wyłączeń ze wspólnych unijnych reguł. A jedną z najbardziej niepopularnych jest swoboda przepływu, czyli prawo m.in. Polaków do osiedlania się i pracy na Zachodzie. GW 27/06/2016, p. 6

For Europe, Brexit will be an event carrying the most repercussions since the Fall of the Berlin Wall. The future direction of events which are now hard to define will largely contradict decisions fuelled by pro-European enthusiasm taken since the fall of the iron curtain. A vote for Brexit would strengthen Eurosceptics and EU opponents in many countries, including e.g. the Netherlands. While blackmailing with referenda on leaving the EU, they would very likely become even more vocal in calls for exemptions from the common EU rules. And one of the most unpopular of those rules is still the freedom of movement one i.e. the right to, among others, the Poles to settle and work in the West.

While the aforementioned Polish liberal discourse remained indeed very broad in terms of deployed arguments and strategies – or combinations thereof – its conservative counter- part seemed particularly limited to one strategy i.e. domesticating Brexit as a logical result of, according to the conservative *Nasz Dziennik* (ND), the anyway profoundly flawed EU project. The thus constructed strongly Eurosceptic discourse of the ND relied in particular on Topos 5 and did so while claiming – somewhat similarly to German conservative discourse about Angela Merkel (above) – that Polish political actors were crucial in causing as well as not avoiding Brexit.

As example 15 shows, the above strategy was achieved via, inter alia, perspectivation achieved through quotes from statements by Jarosław Kaczyński (chairman of the Polish governmental right-wing populist party PiS) expressing usual criticism of his long-term political enemy i.e. the EU council president Donald Tusk. As Kaczyński claimed, Tusk was personally responsible for the EU crisis epitomised by Brexit by having, according to the quote, never offered the British 'anything' and thus driving them out of the EU and causing the current crisis. However, while Tusk was referred to here strictly by means of his name/surname, not functionalising him (i.e. not mentioning his function/role in the EU) was strategic and aimed at degrading him in the statement and in the wider public eye.

EXAMPLE 15:

Prezes PiS stwierdził, że szczególnie ponurą rolę odegrał Donald Tusk, który prowadził rokowania z Brytyjczykami. – W gruncie rzeczy niczego nie otrzymali (…) Ponosi bezpośrednią odpowiedzialność za Brexit i powinien zniknąć z Europejskiej polityki. ND 28/06/2016, p. 6.

PiS Chairman claims that a particularly sombre role has been played by Donald Tusk who led the negotiations with the British. – They essentially have not received anything (…) He is therefore directly responsible for Brexit and should disappear from European politics altogether.

Further to the strategies above, ND discourse also deployed some usual lines of thinking specific for Polish Eurosceptics. While drawing yet again on Topos 5 (European/EU Political and Identity Crisis) in Example 16 it, for example, deployed anti-German arguments – otherwise well-known from the political discourse of the governing PiS – when claiming that the ongoing crisis in the EU was caused by Germany's divisive politics of building a 'hard EU core' ('*twardego jądra UE*'). As it was argued, such strategy had to fail and would not work as many countries – including France, Benelux countries, or countries from southern and northern EU – allegedly opposed such and other Germany-led EU projects thus avoiding Germany's dominance and its alleged EU-hegemony by Germany.

EXAMPLE 16:

Integracja wokół twardego jądra UE zwyczajnie się nie uda. Z dwóch powodów. Po pierwsze kraje Beneluksu, Francja, Południa i kraje skandynawskie nie są gotowe oddać swojego politycznego losu politykom z Berlina. Ze względu na własną sile ekonomiczna Niemcy stworzyłyby wtedy otulinę wokół siebie, która byłaby silnie z nimi zintegrowana. ND 26/06/2016, p. 4.

The integration around the core EU will not work for two reasons. The first of them is that the Benelux countries, France, southern states and the Scandinavian ones are not ready to put their political fate into the hands of politicians from Berlin. Due to its sheer economic power, Germany would then create around itself a strongly integrated buffer zone.

Continuing within the argumentation framed by Topos 5, Polish conservative ND also used further domestication moves by, inter alia, providing criticism of the EU that recontextualised Polish pre-1989 public discourse. As Example 17 shows, the EU was metaphorically compared therein to a 'central committee' ('*Komitet Centralny*') – á la those known from pre-1989 Central and Eastern European ruling communist parties – whereby the EU was historically presupposed to be undemocratic and 'dictating' its member states what to do. The EU was hence shown as allegedly acting against its member states in what was predicated as 'a dangerous way' as was the case with, e.g. the EU refugee quotas during the recent 'refugee crisis'. At the same time, the EU was also criticised for dealing 'with millions of petty things while being unable to deal with the really important ones' ('*zajmuje się milionami nieistotnych spraw a nie potrafi załatwić tych naprawdę ważnych*') thus constructing EU politics as mistaken and trivial.

EXAMPLE 17:

Bruksela wyobraża sobie, że jest takim Komitetem Centralnym, który rozsyła do wszystkich europejskich stolic dyrektywy i polecenia. Są to czasami tak śmieszne kwestie jak – już legendarna – krzywizna banana ale również tak groźne i nieprzemyślane jak przymusowa relokacja imigrantów (…). Bruksela zajmuje się milionami nieistotnych spraw a nie potrafi załatwić tych naprawdę ważnych. ND 28/06/2016, p. 15.

Brussels sees itself as a Central Committee of sorts – such that sends out directives and marching orders to all European capitals. These often concern as ridiculous issues as the by now legendary banana curve but also as dangerous and inconsiderate issues as the forceful relocation of immigrants (…) Brussels deals with millions of petty things while effectively being unable to deal with the really important ones.

3.4.4. Sweden

Finally, though quite unusually for a liberal outlet, Swedish daily *Dagens Nyheter* (DN) focused to large extent on arguments constructed within Topos 4 looking into national and especially international economic crisis already/potentially caused by the Brexit vote. DN opted to consider various options and scenarios for the future while often listing/enumerating either geographical or economic areas (to be) profoundly affected by Brexit. Here, the focus was specifically on the geographical scope of the Brexit-induced crisis with Example 18 enumerating various parts of the globe wherein relevant stock market ('*Tokyo, Paris, Frankfurt, London, New York*') served metonymically as examples of wider economic areas to be affected. By the same token, the example also coined a metaphor that, as a direct repercussion of Brexit, 'the British pound fell through the floor' ('*det brittiska pundet föll igenom golvet*') with overtly nominated economic and market 'fear/anxiety' ('*oro*') also being pointed to as stemming from the Brexit vote and remaining around in a longer run.

EXAMPLE 18:

Britternas nej till EU utlöste chockvågor på världens marknader: Tokyo, Paris, Frankfurt, London, New York. Överallt pekade pilarna nedåt samtidigt som det brittiska pundet föll igenom golvet. Oro finns nu för vad Brexit innebär för Europas ekonomi på längre sikt. DN 25/06/2016, p. 15.

British no to the EU caused a number of shock waves on the world markets: in Tokyo, Paris, Frankfurt, London and New York. Indices fell down overall and the British pound fell through the floor. There is an anxiety as to what Brexit means for European economy in a longer run.

Further to its eagerness towards the economic framing, the Swedish liberal discourse also tended to provide – indeed typically for Swedish press traditional interest in democracy – a relatively extensive look 'on the ground' at the ontology of the Brexit decision in the UK and more specifically within the British constitutional and political as well as democratic crisis (Topos 2). As Example 19 shows, the focus of the foregrounding and activation strategy herewas specifically on the 'British people' ('*Brittiska folket*') who were presupposed to act disruptively for the EU as well as blamed for, as is metaphorically suggested, breaking or causing fracture ('*spräckt*') in the Union. But it is also suggested that such disruptive actions could backfire causing 'fractures in Great Britain' itself via e.g. repercussions of the renewed Scottish claims for independence or Irish claims for reunification.

EXAMPLE 19:

Brittiska folket har spräckt EU. Resultatet av folkomröstningen kan även spräcka Storbritannien. Irländska Sinn Féin vill ha ett enat Irland. I Skottland väcks åter självständighetsfrågan eftersom landet vill stanna i EU. DN 25/06/2016, pp. 8–9.

The British people have now broken the EU. But the result of referendum can also cause a fracture in Great Britain. The Irish Sinn Féin would like to see a unified Ireland. And the independence issue is now again awakened in Scotland which wants to remain in the EU.

However, the democracy focus in the DN was not only achieved via the aforementioned UK-internal perspective but also through a somewhat EU-external one considered from the point of view of the crisis of the EU, its politics and identity (Topos 4; Example 20). Here, however, the foregrounding also eventually turned towards the 'people' while equating the Brexit-supporting 'British' ('*britterna*') with all other 'citizens' ('*medborgarna*') who have lost their trust in the EU. Here, a differentiation strategy was also achieved with the nominated 'elites in Brussels' ('*elit i Bryssel*') clearly juxtaposed with the people/citizens.

EXAMPLE 20:

Många menar dock att britternas nej till EU visar att unionen behöver arbeta för att återupprätta förtroendet bland medborgarna. Ekonomisk kris och arbetslöshet har fått allt fler att skylla på en "elit" i Bryssel som saknar kontakt med folket. DN 25/06/2016, p. 7.

But many think that the British no to the EU shows that the Union needs to work on re-establishing trust among the citizens. The economic crisis and unemployment have caused many to accuse the 'elite' in Brussels of losing touch with the people.

Yet the EU-focussed Topos 4 was not only considered in the Swedish liberal press from the point of view of the current crisis of EU democracy. It was, namely, also used to frame extensive debates about various future scenarios of political action that may help avert, or at least minimise, the more major crisis of European politics. Those scenarios to be taken after Brexit – see Example 21 – were approached metaphorically as different 'ways' ('*vägar*') that the EU could/should be taking within its own realm (e.g. by means of deepening integration) in relations to member states and by means of e.g. responding to the encroaching 'renationalisation' ('*åternationalisering*') taking place in Europe/EU.

EXAMPLE 21:

Tre vägar efter Brexit. Ett alternativ är att fördjupa EU med en klarare befogenhetsfördelning mellan överstaten och medlemsstaterna. Ett andra är att EU blir avsevärt mindre omfattande och att en åternationalisering sker. Det tredje alternativet är att fortsätta att hanka sig fram på inslagen väg DN 26/06/2016, p. 6.

There are three ways after Brexit. One alternative is to deepen the EU with a clear division of power between core and other member states. The other is to make the EU considerably less all-embracing while enabling re-nationalisation. The third one is to continue muddling through on the current path.

On the other hand, the Swedish conservative discourse of the *Svenska Dagbladet* (SvD) followed the pattern of the majority of conservative European press while focusing on, in particular, the economic implications of the UK Brexit referendum. SvD, however, chose to be at least initially less alarmistic and did not, for example, speak of a market or a financial crisis but chose to provide various quasi-anecdotal descriptions of smaller-scale economic implications such as e.g. the so-called 'prosecco panic' that would erupt among Italian winegrowers once the UK market leaves the EU. As was suggested metaphorically/polysemously in Example 22, 'no corks will be popped in Italy if the British vote to leave the EU' ('*Inga korkar kommer smälla i Italien om britterna väljer att lämna EU*').

EXAMPLE 22:

Inga korkar kommer smälla i Italien om britterna väljer att lämna EU. Vinproducenter säger att brexit skulle spricka som en prosecco-bubbla på deras främsta exportmarknad. SvD 24/06/2016, p. 7.

No corks will be popped in Italy if the British choose to leave the EU. Winemakers say that Brexit would make its biggest market burst just like a prosecco-bubble.

But such quasi-anecdotal language – indeed also typical for conservative dailies in other studied countries (see above) – was not the only tone of the Swedish conservative press. Indeed, the SvD also chose to domesticate the Brexit developments very strongly and did so while considering Brexit from the point of view of international economic crisis (Topos 4) that would, it was presupposed, in an obvious way profoundly impact several economies including, very prominently, the Swedish one. Here (see Example 23), argumentation through numbers/examples became prominent as element of, e.g. building analogy that '66000 Swedish jobs are linked to the export to the UK' ('*66 000 svenska jobb är kopplade till exporten till Storbritannien*') and that those jobs are now 'put in danger' ('*står i fara*') as a result of the Brexit vote.

EXAMPLE 23:

Kommerskollegium räknade inför folkomröstningen ut att 66 000 svenska jobb är kopplade till exporten till Storbritannien.- Nu får sysselsättningen definitivt ingen skjuts. Hur stor den negativa effekten blir är svårt att säga. De här 66 000 jobben står i fara SvD 25/06/2016, pp. 6–8.

The National Swedish Board of Trade has counted before the referendum that 66000 Swedish jobs are linked to exports to Great Britain. And now employment certainly gets no boost. It is also difficult to say how big the negative effects will be. But those 66000 jobs are now in danger.

The strong focus on domestication in the conservative Swedish press discourse was also realised by the SvD whenever it chose to build future scenarios of crisis by asking rhetorical questions whether the anti-EU ghosts awaken by the Brexit vote would not gain wider potency beyond just the UK. As was suggested (see Example 24 introduced with an English '*Well …* '), there were many analogies between the UK and Sweden as countries that previously allegedly 'chose to put a brake on the more federalist development of the EU' ('velat bromsa en mer federalistisk utveckling av EU') including by, inter alia, staying out of the Euro area. It was hence suggested that also other EU countries that were not part of the Eurozone – such as Sweden but also, by means of aggregation, other Scandinavian countries like Denmark – could eventually 'disappear' ('försvinner') from the Union or at least have a much 'weaker political influence' ('få ett svagare politiskt inflytande') in the future.

EXAMPLE 24:

Well - både Sverige och Storbritannien har ju också gemensamt velat bromsa en mer federalistisk utveckling av EU. Ett exempel på detta är att båda länderna har stått utanför eurosamarbetet. Och när det mäktiga Storbritannien försvinner är det möjligt att EU-länder utan den gemensamma valutan - som Sverige och Danmark - kommer att få ett svagare politiskt inflytande i unionen. SvD 26/06/2016, pp. 14–15.

Well – both Sweden and Great Britain have chosen to stop a more federalist development of the EU. One example is that both countries have remained outside the Euro collaboration. But when the powerful Great Britain disappears, it is likely that the EU countries outside the common currency – such as Sweden or Denmark – will have a much weaker political influence in the EU.

4. Conclusions

The above analysis shows clearly that the UK 2016 vote to leave the European Union was – contrary to the UK public sphere which largely undermined the critical tones – perceived across the European public sphere as both a current and a future crisis. As has been shown in the course of examination of the Austrian, German, Polish and Swedish media, both liberal and conservative European press recognised a far-reaching, negative and indeed critical impact of the Brexit vote and considered its importance as crisis within an array of dimensions that were UK-specific, international and European (see Figure 2). Those dimensions also nested the key argumentative resources – i.e. *topoi* – which allowed, albeit in an often-differentiated manner, to construct the arguments about, inter alia, economic, social and political/democratic implications of Brexit along with its relevance to the UK, EU and indeed internationally/globally. They all formed a specific semantic field of the 'Brexit' concept as attached to various formats and dimensions of 'crisis' in the studied discourses nested within both wider and nationally-specific tendencies in reporting crisis and its implications for politics, society and the economy.

As the analysis indicates, the imaginary of crisis was very strongly attached to the European media representations and interpretations of the UK Brexit vote. The key aspect of such discursive constructions of 'Brexit as crisis' imaginary was, as was hypothesised above, in building a very peculiar past-to-future connection. Hence, practically irrespective of the fact whether provided by the liberal or conservative media, the analysed discourse not only pointed to the past/current ontologies of the British decision to vote in favour of Brexit but also painted a vast array of scenarios of future crises (soon to be) caused by UK decision to leave the EU. The very powerful aspect of building that link resided in the fact that it connected the experience – or any otherwise understood 'real' and lived facts about EU, European politics, etc – with expectations about its future developments that will be profoundly distorted, if not altogether averted, by the Brexit vote. The crisis scenario-building was, as was expected above, also made real by recontextualising the experience of various social/political/economic crises and projecting (aspects of) those on the de facto description of Brexit which was thus *pre-legitimised* as one of the most significant critical occurrences in the post-War European history.

Further to the above, the other key transversal aspect of the analysed media discourse was also that, again irrespectively of their liberal or conservative provenance, the analysed discursive representations showed a strong tendency to domesticate the Brexit debates and to consider the latter's critical implications in particular from the point of view of studied national public spheres and politics/societies. While such a domestication occurred at various levels – ranging from international economy, through European and national politics/society to specific 'people' and social groups or even individuals affected by the Brexit in the UK and elsewhere – it very clearly showed that the focal 'Brexit as crisis' connection was in most cases debated in terms of its implication for specific national public spheres including their own perceptions of both national and transnational spaces such as, e.g. the European politics.

However, as has been shown in the course of the above analysis, several tendencies could be observed that were cross-national rather than just nationally-specific in nature and often constituted a relative novelty given traditional interests of the liberal or conservative media. These included, inter alia, the very strong tendency of the liberal press to remain pro-European as well as consider the Brexit vote from a variety of (national incl. UK and international or European) perspectives and lines of interpretation (via different topoi). The liberal press also in most cases focussed on political and social dimensions and implications of the UK referendum rather than on its economic repercussions. On the other hand, it could be seen that the conservative press displayed some rather unanimous tendency to focus on the market/economic implications of the UK referendum and of the eventual Brexit. It did so while very often avoiding discussing social and political implications of the UK vote and while increasingly recontextualising both cross-national and domestic 'quasi-realistic' Eurosceptic tones epitomised by e.g. the peculiar *'Schaden-freude'* discourse in relation to the alleged failures of the EU-ropean project.

Disclosure statement

No potential conflict of interest was reported by the author.

References

Adler-Nissen, R., Galpin, C., & Rosamond, B. (2017). Performing Brexit: How a post-Brexit world is imagined outside the United Kingdom. *The British Journal of Politics and International Relations*, *19*(3), 573–591.

Alasuutari, P., Qadir, A., & Creutz, K. (2013). The domestication of foreign news: News stories related to the 2011 Egyptian revolution in British, Finnish and Pakistani newspapers. *Media, Culture & Society*, *35*(6), 692–707.

Bromley, M., & Slavtcheva-Petkova, V. (2019). *Global journalism: An introduction*. Basingstoke: Palgrave.

Clausen, L. (2004). Localizing the global: 'Domestication' processes in international news production. *Media, Culture & Society*, *26*(1), 25–44.

Cottle, S. (2009). *Global crisis reporting*. Maidenhead: Open University Press.

Evans, G., & Menon, A. (2017). *Brexit and British politics*. Cambridge: Polity Press.

Galtung, J., & Rugge, M. H. (1965). The structure of foreign news: The presentation of the Congo, Cuba and Cyprus Crises in four Norwegian newspapers. *Journal of Peace Research*, *2*(1), 64–90.

Graham, P. (2019). Negative discourse analysis and Utopias of the political. *Journal of Language and Politics*, *18*(1). doi:10.1075/jlp.18052.gra

Gurevitch, M., & Levy, M. (1990). The global newsroom. *British Journalism Review*, *2*(2), 27–37.

Hall, S., Critcher, C., Jefferson, T., Clarke, J., & Roberts, B. (1978). *Policing the crisis*. London: Macmillan.

Hannerz, U. (2004). *Foreign news*. Chicago, IL: The University of Chicago Press.

Jessop, B. (2015). Crisis construal in the North Atlantic financial crisis and the Eurozone crisis. *Competition & Change*, *19*(2), 95–112.

Koller, V., Kopf, S., & Miglbauer, M. (Eds.). (2019). *Discourses of Brexit*. London: Routledge.

Koopmans, R., & Erbe, J. (2004). Towards a European public sphere? Vertical and horiziontal dimensions of Europeanized political communication. *Innovation*, *17*(2), 97–118.

Koopmans, R., & Statham, P. (Eds.). (2009). *The making of a European public sphere*. Cambridge: CUP.

Koselleck, R. (1979). *Critique and crisis*. Cambridge, MA: MIT Press.

Koselleck, R. (2002). *The practice of conceptual history*. Stanford, CA: Stanford University Press.

Koselleck, R. (2004). *Futures past: On the semantics of historical time*. New York, NY: Columbia University Press.

Koselleck, R. (2006). Crisis. *Journal of the History of Ideas*, *67*(2), 357–400.

Krzyżanowska, N., & Krzyżanowski, M. (2018). 'Crisis' and migration in Poland: Discursive shifts, anti-pluralism, and the politicisation of exclusion. *Sociology*, *52*(3), 612–618.

Krzyżanowski, M. (2009). Europe in crisis: Discourses on crisis-events in the European press 1956–2006. *Journalism Studies*, *10*(1), 18–35.

Krzyżanowski, M. (2010). *The discursive construction of European identities*. Frankfurt: Peter Lang.

Krzyżanowski, M. (2012). (Mis) communicating Europe? On deficiencies and challenges in political and institutional communication in the European Union. In B. Kryk-Kastovsky (Ed.), *Intercultural miscommunication past and present* (pp. 185–213). Frankfurt: Peter Lang.

Krzyżanowski, M. (2014). Values, imaginaries and templates of journalistic practice: A critical discourse analysis. *Social Semiotics*, *24*(3), 345–365.

Krzyżanowski, M. (2016). Recontextualisation of neoliberalism and the increasingly conceptual nature of discourse: Challenges for critical discourse studies. *Discourse & Society*, *27*(3), 308–321.

Krzyżanowski, M. (2018). Discursive shifts in ethno-nationalist politics: On politicisation and mediatisation of the 'refugee crisis' in Poland. *Journal of Immigrant & Refugee Studies*, *16*(1–2), 76–96.

Krzyżanowski, M., Triandafyllidou, A., & Wodak, R. (2009). Europe, media, crisis and the European public sphere: Conclusions. In A. Triandafyllidou, R. Wodak, & M. Krzyżanowski (Eds.), *The European public sphere and the media: Europe in crisis* (pp. 261–268). Basingstoke: Palgrave Macmillan.

Krzyżanowski, M., Triandafyllidou, A., & Wodak, R. (2018). The politicisation and mediatisation of the refugee crisis in Europe: Discursive practices and legitimation strategies. *Journal of Immigrant & Refugee Studies*, *16*(1–2), 1–14.

Krzyżanowski, M., & Wodak, R. (2011). Political strategies and language policies: The 'rise and fall' of the EU Lisbon strategy and its implications for the union's multilingualism policy. *Language Policy*, *10*(2), 115–136.

Levitas, R. (2011). *The concept of Utopia*. Witney: Peter Lang.

Levitas, R. (2014). *Utopia as method*. Basingstoke: Palgrave Macmillan.

O'Toole, F. (2018). *Heroic failure: Brexit and the politics of pain*. London: Head of Zeus.

Raboy, M., & Dagenais, B. (1992). *Media, crisis and democracy*. London: Sage.

Reisigl, M., & Wodak, R. (2001). *Discourse & discrimination*. London: Routledge.

Richardson, J. E. (2007). *Analysing newspapers*. Basingstoke: Palgrave Macmillan.

Ridge-Newman, A., Leon-Solis, F., & O'Donnell, H. (Eds.). (2018). *Reporting the road to Brexit*. Basingstoke: Palgrave Macmillan.

Schlesinger, P. (1991). *Media, state and the nation*. London: Sage.

Street, J. (2011). *Mass media, politics and democracy*. Basingstoke: Palgrave Macmillan.

Sum, N.-L., & Jessop, B. (2013). *Towards a cultural political economy*. Cheltenham: Edward Elgar.

Taylor, C. (2004). *Modern social imaginaries*. Durham, NC: Duke University Press.

Triandafyllidou, A., Wodak, R., & Krzyżanowski, M. (eds.). (2009). *The European public sphere and the media: Europe in crisis*. Basingstoke: Palgrave Macmillan.

van Leeuwen, T. (2007). Legitimation in discourse and communication. *Discourse & Communication, 1*(1), 91–112.

van Leeuwen, T. (2008). *Discourse and practice*. Cambridge: CUP.

Wodak, R. (2001). The discourse historical approach. In R. Wodak & M. Meyer (Eds.), *Methods of critical discourse analysis* (pp. 63–95). London: Sage.

Wodak, R., & Angouri, J. (2014). From Grexit to Grecovery: Euro/crisis discourses. *Discourse & Society*, *25*(4), 417–423.

Wodak, R., & Krzyżanowski, M. (2017). Right-wing populism in Europe and the USA. *Journal of Language and Politics, 16*(4), 471–484.

Wolin, S. (1989). *The presence of the past*. Baltimore, MB: The Johns Hopkins University Press.

Wolin, S. (2004). *Politics and vision: Continuity and innovation in Western political thought*. Princeton, NJ: Princeton University Press.

Wolin, S. (2008). *Democracy Inc.: Managed democracy and the spectre of inverted totalitarianism*. Princeton, NJ: Princeton University Press.

Index